Skeletal Scramble

Skeletal Scramble

by

Katherine Traphagen

All characters, places, events, and situations in this story are
purely fictional. Any resemblance to reality is coincidental.

About the Book

To protest the museum's continued possession of Wampanoag skeletons, a Native American activist makes a bold statement. Dr. Caleb Russell Emerson, one of the museum's most noted archaeologists, receives a package and embarks upon a clandestine project. Eric, the night watchman at the museum's storehouse, begins a secret mission to rescue the bones of his Wampanoag ancestors.

Susan, the new administrator at the museum's storehouse, is afraid she is going to lose her job, if not her mind. She is certain someone is moving the useless relics in the storehouse around, but she can't imagine who or why.

Will they ever straighten it all out?

Dedication

I would especially like to thank my parents for their support and encouragement. Also, thanks to Mary Lou Godleski for being my genealogy mentor, and to my good friend, Michelle Black for helping me put it all together.

Chapter One

The waitress was rude. There was no other way to take it. She was stout and ageless with limp mousy hair. First, she ignored them as long as possible, maybe hoping they would leave. When she finally had to speak to them, she was cold and short. She took their order grudgingly and brought their food as though she were glad to be rid of it.

The diner was small and simple, but Eric usually liked it here. It was just off the highway, so it was convenient. He preferred giving a little business to locally owned restaurants rather than the national chains. The diner's decor was nothing to write home about, but that was what gave a dive its charm. The food here was good and there was plenty of it.

The waitress stopped to check on another table before she sat down behind the counter. Her attitude toward the other customers was pleasant and polite. Clearly, this was personal, not just a bad mood.

Eric kept his cool. After all, he did not need to put up with this treatment very often. It was only times like this when he was with his sister, Melissa, that he had to deal with this attitude. He could get past it. It was more important to have lunch and enjoy his sister's company than to dwell on a stranger's ignorance.

To look at them, no one would ever jump to the conclusion that they were brother and sister. In fact, it would have been difficult to find better opposites to compare.

Eric Larson was tall and muscular. Despite his blond hair, he tanned pretty well. The exception was his nose which was slightly scorched, contrasting with clear elfish green eyes.

Eric had a truck and Harley. The Harley was an important piece of his identity. Usually, keeping with the image, he dressed like he had just walked off the construction site. Silently, he prided himself in being a laid-back kind of guy.

Melissa Larson Brown was short and curvaceous rather than plump. Glossy black hair framed her round face. She tanned a deep copper tone shade. Her clothes changed with her mood, and her emotional state was always an open book.

Melissa loved comfort and beauty. Her house was decorated luxuriously. Every seat had an extra pillow, and every corner had an artistic touch to it.

Once you knew their heritage, the difference in appearance was easily understood. Each of their parents was half Scandinavian and half Native American. While Eric looked very Swedish, Melissa looked very Wampanoag. The other three siblings were variations in between.

Judging from her manner toward them, the waitress was presuming they were a mixed race couple. Her rudeness was an expression of her disapproval. Privately, Eric found it almost amusing, but across the table he could see Melissa fuming.

"Come on," he urged gently. "Let's get past it, Sis."

"I know," Melissa sighed. "I know it's pointless, but I just didn't need this today."

"The important thing is that we're together, right?"

"Barely together..."

"Is it Rad?" Eric knew it was Rad. When Melissa had problems, her husband was usually at the root of it. It was too bad, because Eric liked Rad even though he was the radical his nickname implied.

"Of course, it's Steve," Melissa said, using her husband's actual name. "He's gone totally off the deep end again."

"Drinking?" Eric asked expectantly.

"No," Melissa denied. "Surprise of surprises, he's not drinking."

"Then what this time?" Eric asked.

"He's immersed himself in Tribal politics," Melissa explained. "All he does is read laws and treaties and go to meetings. He goes on and on, ranting to me about how awful the world is to us - like I don't know anything about it. He's driving me crazy."

"I thought you wanted him to stop drinking and do something meaningful."

"I meant get a job!" Melissa cried indignantly.

Eric laughed. "You knew Steve was a rad when you married

him. What'd you expect?"

Melissa knew when she was being baited. Fair was fair.

"Okay, if that's how you feel about it," Melissa countered. "Do you know he didn't want me to have dinner with you tonight?"

"Huhn?" Eric was shocked. "Are you serious, Sis?"

"Oh, absolutely serious."

"Why not?"

"Because of your job," Melissa said as if the connection were obvious. She was glad the guys were friends, but Eric didn't appreciate what she put up with from Steve.

"My job? At the museum?" Eric couldn't imagine what bearing that could have on anything.

"I told you," Melissa warned. "He has totally immersed himself in Tribal politics."

"But, what could be wrong with the museum?" Eric asked.

"You don't have any idea?" Melissa just had to try and make him guess.

Eric frowned, thinking it over. "Their exhibits are okay. I've seen all of them, and they're pretty factual. I'm not insulted by them."

"It's not the exhibits - it's the skeletons."

"Skeletons?"

"The skeletons," Melissa said emphatically. "Don't you know about the skeletons?"

"No, I don't. What skeletons?"

"There are eight Native American skeletons that the museum is holding on to," Melissa explained.

"The law says they have to return those."

"To nationally recognized tribes. We aren't nationally recognized, so he could be right about that."

"Sis, I haven't seen any skeletons there, and I am the security guard..."

Melissa rolled her eyes. "Last night, for three hours, Steve the radical yelled at me, because you work in a place with less than a dozen skeletons still in storage. Do I deserve that? Is it my fault? I'm telling you, this is worse than the time he invited the UFO's to land on the back forty."

"That was fun," Eric objected just to bait her, "kicking back, drinking tequila, waiting for the aliens to land..."

"Oh, stop it!" Melissa snapped with disgust. "You're as bad as he is."

Eric laughed. He loved teasing his favorite sister.

"Miss, Do you still love him?" he asked seriously.

Melissa considered it. "Yes, I still love him, but this time I'm really worried about the kind of trouble he could get into. It's different than his usual crackpot theories. He's talking about hiding out in Maine or maybe Canada after he does whatever it is he's going to do."

Eric was started taking her seriously. "What is he going to do?"

"That's just it," Melissa was starting to feel weepy with worry. "I don't know - he says he doesn't want me implicated."

"That does have an ominous ring to it," Eric admitted.

"I know it does." Melissa's eyes welled up with tears. "All he'll tell me is that everything hinges on the decisions made at the next council meeting. If it doesn't go his way, he's going to execute the 'Hillman Plan.' I have no idea what he's talking about. What could the 'Hillman Plan' possibly be?"

Eric pondered for a minute. It worried him too, but what could be done? Rad would do what Rad would do.

"Don't get too upset, Sis," he advised. "After all, look at Steve's track record. The FBI phone tap was a loose cord, right?"

Melissa smiled a bit. "True."

"And the alien implant was just a mole, wasn't it?"

"I forgot about that..." Melissa giggled.

"Odds are this 'Hillman Plan' will be just as dramatic and come to nothing. Why don't you sit back and enjoy the ride like the rest of us?"

First Melissa sighed, and then she laughed. "You're right. It's a good thing I married a nut case. What else would we do for entertainment?"

Eric laughed too. "You know, he gets carried away, but he does make you think. I ought to check into that skeleton thing. I hope that's not true. It would bother me."

"Maybe you shouldn't," Melissa cautioned. "You like that job."

"Yeah, it is a cool job..."

"You know, we came here to talk about you. How are you?"

"Okay."

"I mean, how are you without Astrid?" Melissa knew Eric. He always said he was at least okay, no matter how bad he was really feeling. He had been living with Astrid for over a year when she suddenly left. Melissa knew he had to be upset about it no matter what he said to the contrary.

"Well, I miss her if that's what you mean," Eric acknowledged.

"I mean, how upset are you?" Melissa pried.

"I don't really know yet," he said quietly. "I've been trying to keep busy."

"Why did she leave?"

"That's just it. I don't exactly know," Eric shrugged. "She sent a long letter saying it wasn't about me. She was going back to Sweden, because she was homesick. According to her, there's nothing to talk about."

"How about according to you?" Eventually, Melissa knew she could get him to talk.

"I'm still confused. I don't know quite what to think yet."

"Why don't you go after her? Uncle Sig would help you find a job if you wanted to stay."

"No," Eric said. "I considered it for a while, especially right at first, but I don't think that's such a good idea."

"Why not?"

"Because," Eric admitted painfully, "I'm not sure she wants me to. She didn't ask me to go with her."

"Did you have any kind of a fight?" Melissa persisted.

"No," Eric denied. "I'm telling you, I've been over it in my head again and again. As far as I can tell, everything was fine, right up until she packed her bags and left me."

"Was she depressed? I mean about missing home?"

"Not that I noticed... She did start sleeping a lot, and she got weepy over a couple little things, but nothing serious happened. That's what I don't understand."

Melissa considered the situation. "Maybe she was really homesick for quite a while and didn't let on."

"Oh, I doubt that," Eric said quickly. "Astrid isn't one to keep her feelings to herself."

Melissa laughed. "You're right! What was I saying? I've never met anyone who complained so much!"

"Hey, remember that week after the hurricane? She went on all week because the power was out. Then when it came back on she said it more romantic without the lights."

The waitress intruded with the check. Ignoring the dirty dishes, she turned to walk away.

"No, wait," Eric stopped her. "I've got it right here." He pulled a bill out of his pocket and handed it to the waitress. "Dinner's on me, Sis."

The waitress stopped dead. "Sister? She's your sister?"

"Yeah."

The waitress looked from one to the other incredulously. "Your real sister? Are you sure?"

The two siblings laughed heartily and left.

Joe Green poured a cup of coffee, and then he wished he hadn't. He was trying to switch over to tea or water or herbal tea. They were better for his nerves and his stomach. Today was a rainy day, and coffee seemed more warming to him. That still did not justify his choice, but he let it go anyway.

His office was not showy, but it was functional and comfortable. It was in an old building, which had its good and bad points to it. The elevators were slow and occasionally jammed. Everything always looked worn and a little dirty. The plus side was that the windows opened and let in real fresh air. The ornate fixtures and woodwork lent an air of elegance missing in modern designs.

His job was working for the Wampanoag Nation. He managed tribal business, lobbied with politicians and bureaucrats, coordinated meetings, dealt with the Bureau of Indian Affairs, and handled special projects.

Admittedly, there was more money elsewhere, but he

preferred to work for his people. For one thing there was a certain amount of prestige and respect within the tribe for him. For another thing, it was personally gratifying and fulfilling to be making social progress for the people. Besides all of that, he liked not being the only Native American.

At first glance, most people did not peg him as a Native American. He had straight dark hair and brown eyes. His facial features were typical among his people, although they were not recognized as typically Native American. Asian Indian and Eastern European were the most common guesses. He was much happier not having to explain his heritage.

One of his special projects was a search to find a set of missing Wampanoag relics, the Wampum Belts. Wampum was colorful shells used as currency before the Europeans arrived. The Wampum Belts were beadwork showing the pictorial history of the people. There were three belts, worn by the Wampanoag Kings on special occasion. The belts were rumored by legend to be spectacular. Not only were they made of money, but the workmanship and the beauty were breathtaking.

Over three hundred years age, during King Philip's War with the English settlers, the Wampum Belts were captured by the English. The ranking officer, Captain Benjamin Church, turned them over to Edward Winslow, the Governor of Massachusetts Colony. Protocol required they be turned over to the Crown.

Waldergrave Pelham, the Governor's brother-in-law was entrusted to take the Wampum Belts to England. Three years later, King Charles II denied having ever received them. The Wampum Belts were never seen again.

Locating them after all of this time seemed like a hopeless task. Still Joe had to try something. He felt it was unlikely that King Charles would lie about receiving the Wampum Belts. Why would he? Reasoning, that one of the other principles or someone close to them must have taken the Wampum Belts, he found a starting point.

What would you do with them? You could take them apart and use the Wampum. But even a dumb person would realize that the Belts were worth more intact than broken up. You could not sell or trade them without rumors starting. Who would buy them? This sort of relic did not have a big underground market.

They could have been kept as spoils of war. Anyone in the Governor's Office or inner circle would have had a chance to abscond with them. They could still exist. It was possible someone had them and did not know what they were. Of course anywhere along the way someone could have thrown them out without knowing what they were. He did not like to think about that possibility.

Hopefully, they had been passed down through the family of the purloiner until present day. This was where the genealogist came in. Joe felt the best chance they had was to follow the lines of inheritance of some of the more likely suspects. The best person to do that was a genealogist.

Okay, it was still an incredible long shot, but at least there was a chance. The important point was that he was doing something. Besides, you never knew until you tried.

The genealogist he selected was Ellen Bradley. She had done a lot of research tracing local families back through the colonial eras. Ellen was not the frail elderly lady he had expected. She was vibrant, talkative, and only slightly gray.

Joe drank his coffee as he organized. Automatically, he began to pour more, then he stopped. He needed to call Ellen and prepare for their meeting. Worse yet, Rad was on his way over. He had a lot to do, and jittering would not help.

First, he decided to call Ellen and check on the genealogy project. Her last message sounded like she was excited about something.

He picked up the phone and dialed Ellen's number.

"Hello."

"Hi, Ellen, it's Joe. How are you?"

"I meant to call you," she said hesitantly. "But I got hung up with research."

Her tone was friendly, but Joe felt she was hedging.

"Happens to us all," he replied.

"I'm so close..." she trailed off. How could she tell him the real reason she hadn't made any progress?

"But not there yet?" Joe finished for her. This was frustrating. Although he hadn't exactly gone out on a limb on this project, he was spending some money on it. Progress would have been very reassuring.

"Well, right, exactly." Silently, Ellen cursed herself for oversleeping this week. Here she was, putting off her best client, because she had fallen in love. If only she could actually have gone to bed earlier instead of staying up late talking and smootching...

Ellen had answered a little too quickly. Joe could tell she was putting him off, so he got to the point. "Do you have anything concrete for me to take to the meeting?"

"Uumm, no, but I'm sure there will be soon." Ellen tried not to sound desperate. She just could not afford to lose Joe. He was one of the few clients that actually paid her on time. "I know I'm close. I can just feel it."

"Okay." Joe heard her apology through her words, and he was appeased.

Ellen felt the need to explain, except of course for the truth. "You know, I told you in the beginning that this was an off the wall project for me, which is great. It's actually coming along okay, but genealogical research is slow under the best of conditions. I just couldn't get to the documents I needed today."

"Well keep at it," Joe cut in on her babbling. "Let me know when you get something."

"Definitely, I'll call you immediately."

Joe was disappointed, but at least he had a while to look over the business for the meeting. It would be all the same difficult issues such as scholarships, housing, and health care. Privately, he thought of them as 'the headache issues.' Hopefully he could get something lighter on the agenda like language and cultural preservation. Everyone seemed to brighten up and enjoy that part.

Just as Joe got focused, Rad appeared in his doorway. Rad was a large man. He was dark with heavy features. The timing was bad, but Joe did not want to appear ungracious.

"Come on in."

Rad bounded in carrying two large cups and a bag from Dunkin' Donuts. He set them on the desk with flourish.

"Hey, Joe," Rad said happily. "I know you like Dunkin'

Donuts' coffee. Since I'm here to chew your ear, I wanted to do something nice for you."

"Thanks, Steve," Joe replied hesitantly. As hard as he was trying to break the habit, he could not turn down the gift. Besides, if he read the signs right, he was going to need the coffee to keep up with Rad. "Why don't you sit down, relax, and tell me what's on your mind."

"I can't sit..." Rad paced waving his arms. "I can't wait, and I can't relax. I need to dive in, because I just can't deal with the complacency any more."

Joe had a bad feeling he should not ask, but he did. "What complacency?"

"Of our people," Rad replied as though it were obvious. "We sit here and accept every raw deal handed to us. It's got to stop. A statement needs to be made."

Joe sighed silently. Steve was being radioactive Rad again. They had known each other since middle school. Steve was brilliant, and Joe admired his zeal, but it was exhausting. "Have you been going to the Council meetings?"

"Yes, I've gone to three of them," Rad said bitterly. "They were long. They were boring, and nothing happened. I have to make something happen."

"What are you going to do?" Joe wondered if he should worry. Steve always meant well, but he did get carried away.

"I'm going to go to the next meeting to stand up and speak my mind." Steve declared.

Now Joe worried. "The first half of the meeting is open to everyone, but what are you going to say?"

"What I just said to you," Rad said proudly. "No more complacency! They've been doing nothing while we need action. Things have to change, even if I have to do it myself!"

So that was why Rad had come to him. He needed to be stopped. "That should alienate everyone," Joe commented.

"You don't think I should say that?" Steve said with surprise.

"No."

"Isn't the open part of the meeting for speaking your mind?"

"Go ahead, but venting won't get anything done. Now sit

down here because I want to tell you something." Joe looked Rad right in the eye until he sat. "While you've been floating around tequila bottles, talking to aliens, and searching for Elvis, the rest of us have been working for health care, scholarships, and jobs. It takes a lot of audacity for you to come in here and say we're complacent and you're not happy with the job we're doing. Change just doesn't come in one felt swoop. It's hard tedious work."

Rad looked like he had been slapped. "I never thought about it that way." He had not expected this reaction.

"You're the new kid on the block here," Joe explained. "Don't start off acting like you know everything. We all know you're smart and your heart's in the right place. Just tone it down."

Rad fidgeted while he thought about it. This was good advice, really good advice. He had forgotten how things looked from the outside. The cause needed to come before his own frustration. "Why don't you help me out with this, Joe?"

"Why don't you start slow," Joe advised. "Begin by volunteering for a committee and a few activities?"

Rad hesitated and thought for a minute. He knew it would not be wise to reveal all of his plans to Joe. What was he really trying to do by talking at the meeting? Assess the mood of the people, maybe? He needed action, preferably with lots of the people. If not, there was the 'Hillman Plan.'

"Joe, I still feel I have to say something tomorrow."

"What's the issue bothering you the most?"

"Complacency," Rad replied.

That figured. Why did he ask? "What's the issue bothering you next to the most?"

"Our heritage," Rad said sadly. "No one cares about it anymore."

"Yes, we do," Joe contradicted. He rarely lost his temper, but if anyone could drive him to it, it was Steve.

"Then where are the Wampum belts?" Rad demanded. "The history of our people has been missing for over three hundred years. What's being done to get them back? Why are our ancestors' skeletons still being held by museums? We should lay their bones to rest in the Earth and run our own museum. Then if anyone really wants to know about our culture, they'll get the answer from us. How many people speak our language? Why aren't we speaking it together right now?"

"Hold it!" Joe interrupted. He had listened to this ranting long enough. "The reason we're not speaking our language is because you don't know it! Before you bring that up, you better learn it. Not only that you'd better get caught up. I've been conscientiously sending letters to museums about our skeletons. As far as the Wampum Belts, I'm trying out a new approach, but it may take a long time."

"That's not good enough," Rad said standing his ground. "We need action now!"

"What do you want to do?" Joe asked.

"Protests," Rad began. "Rally, petitions..."

"Stop," Joe interrupted. "Steve, I threw away my love beads, and so did everybody else."

"If you don't demand anything, you don't get anything," Rad said earnestly. "Why do you think we're constantly being overlooked? It's because we're reasonable. We don't insist. We let them walk over us."

"Rad," Joe reminded. "You know it's not that easy. Whether you see it or not, we're making progress by doing things the way we're doing them. If and when you must speak at the meeting, keep that in mind."

"I'll try," Rad promised. He was finding it difficult to deal with this and not reveal the 'Hillman Plan.' "I'll really try, but I've still got to make my point. We need to take action to keep our heritage alive. If we don't shake things up soon, it'll be too late."

"Then what do you want from me?"

"Help me out." Steve sincerely wanted to try motivation first. "So that the people will listen to me."

Susan Slater caught a look at herself in the mirror. Her blue suit was too bright. It was only a shade too bright, but it triggered all of her insecurities. All week, she had worried about it. Now that she was already at the office on her first day of work, she was certain it was all wrong.

She should have stuck with navy or brown, but her eyes were an off shade of blue and navy looked wrong. Her hair was a mousey shade of blond, so brown looked wrong too.

It was too late now. Her new boss, Joshua Moorland was there. He was tall, gray, and ruddy with an air of formality. His suit was impeccable.

"How about if we begin with an introductory tour?" He asked in a friendly tone, but Susan still felt a little overwhelmed.

"Th-that-that would be great," she stammered.

Joshua held the door open for her. She was exactly what he wanted for this job. Polite, pleasant, and insecure, he knew she would be easy to deal with. Although it was listed under administration, the job was really a flunky position. He wanted to get some of the crummy projects like inventory and procedures out of the way. Some knowledge of archaeology and management was necessary, otherwise he would have hired an undergraduate student.

"The first person you need to meet here is Jeannie," Joshua said gesturing to the woman behind the front desk. "Jeannie's officially my personal secretary, but in reality, she's more like the department editor. Everything of any importance around here goes through her."

Jeannie was a heavy woman with a studious air. She looked up impassively over her half glasses. "Pleased to meet you."

"Likewise..." Susan began.

"You'll have plenty of time to get to know each other later," Joshua interrupted as he motioned her onwards.

He led her down a dim corridor and stairway to a dingy corridor. "All of the buildings are connected by underground tunnels like this. It's very convenient in the winter."

"It looks very old," Susan commented hesitantly.

"Oh yes, it is," Joshua agreed heartily. "The museum does its best to conserve its funds and resources as well as to preserve the architectural integrity of the buildings and artifacts it's been entrusted with."

Casting a stray glance into a dark corner, Susan thought she saw something move. She hurried through the door Joshua was holding for her.

"This," Joshua announced, "is the building you'll be working in."

The building was old and needed paint if not new dry wall. The halls turned and twisted like a maze. Still, it was an improvement over the tunnel.

"The first person you have to meet over here is Eric," Joshua said.

Eric nodded courteously. Susan seemed out of place to him. She looked altogether too timid and polite.

"Eric is our weekend night security person," Joshua continued. "You won't see much of him. He's usually off duty during the day."

"Pleased to meet you," Susan said. She was terribly nervous. Already, she had forgotten the guard's name. Joshua was already opening another door, and now she could not ask.

"This is Dr. Caleb Russell Emerson," Joshua introduced. "You'll be taking over many of the administrative duties he's shouldered up until now."

"Dr. Emerson," Susan greeted as she entered his office.

"Yes, come in," the man inside said busily. Dr. Emerson was a tall thin man in his fifties with graying hair, sharp features and ice blue eyes. His clothes were elegant, but rumpled. He searched through the scattered papers on top of his desk for a moment, and then he looked up at them. "It's a pleasure to meet you." He went back to searching his desk.

"This is Ms. Susan Slater," Joshua introduced casually. "She's our new administrator."

"Right, right... There's a list here..." Caleb muttered still ignoring them. He picked up a glass of water with a plant growing in it and drank from it.

"There's a plant in there," Susan exclaimed.

Both men glanced at her quizzically as if she had said something nonsensical.

"I'll refill it later," Dr. Emerson replied absently. For the first time, he sized up Susan and surmised that Joshua had made a fine choice. She was visibly nervous and trying hard to be agreeable. These duties clearly belonged to a person with a more agreeable temperament than his own.

"Now, as I was saying," Dr. Emerson said pleasantly. "I have compiled a list of duties I'm officially turning over to you, Susan. I'll have the files sent over later." He handed a list on a clipboard to Susan and an envelope to Joshua. "It's all just as we discussed, Joshua."

"Good, good," Joshua said smoothly. "We'll be running along now. I haven't even shown Susan her office yet.

Joshua led Susan back into the lobby.

"Dr. Emerson is a little eccentric," Joshua explained. "But he's a very brilliant archaeologist. We're privileged to have him on our staff. In fact, your position was created largely to allow him to devote himself fully to research and writing. Let me show you your office."

Susan felt vaguely ignored and disoriented. She had the odd feeling there was something no one was telling her. Just to add to her confusion, they had to go deep into the maze to get to her office.

"We still have quite a few things stored in here," Joshua explained as he opened the door. "However since you are in charge of all of it now, we felt that wouldn't be a problem."

The room appeared to be jam packed with boxes, desks and files. It was painted peach, probably from the fifties and had a tile floor. The window looked out at a brick wall, but at least it was a window.

"Here's your computer." Joshua graciously motioned to a box on the floor. "And here's your list of duties and objectives. Why don't you take the rest of the day to get settled in here. If there's anything you need, just tell Jeannie about it in the morning. I have to be off to a meeting now."

"Okay," Susan replied as he left. As she surveyed the office, she began to feel a little overwhelmed. It was so bleak and cold. A rug and a lamp would warm it up. Maybe she could find another place for the desks, boxes, and clutter.

She skimmed the lists. They pretty well agreed with each other. Her primary duties were to supervise personnel, keep staff procedures up to date, see to building maintenance, set up the new computer, and input the storehouse collection catalog. Suddenly she wished she had not grossly exaggerated her computer skills.

Chapter Two

Joe stifled another yawn. He was afraid his jaw would break if he yawned any harder. Why had he resisted a cup of coffee before the meeting? He knew what meetings were like. No matter where he scheduled them, the room was always warm and dim. During the beginning, the Elders sat at a table or on a stage. He sat inconspicuously at the front of the crowd. It was hard not to doze off.

Joe shifted uncomfortably and tried to pay attention. Council meetings always ran at least until nine o'clock. After spending most of last night helping Rad, he was not sure he could stay awake that long.

Lilly, his assistant saw him dozing. She was disgusted. It was disgraceful for the representative to sleep during a Council meeting. It was her duty to keep him awake no matter what. First, she glared at him. Finding that ineffective, she nudged him. Now, it was Rad's turn to speak. Just to make sure Joe stayed awake, Lilly kicked him with the spike of her heel.

Joe jumped as her heel dug into his leg. He looked directly into her stern black eyes and then sat up straight looking toward where Rad was sitting.

Rad stood up slowly and looked at the rest of the audience. Some he knew, and some he did not. Most looked marginally concerned or even bored. He was psyched to speak and could not wait to motivate them and see fight and enthusiasm surface.

The Elder nodded at him, and his stomach flip-flopped unexpectedly. He thought he was prepared, but now he was trembling and his mind had gone blank.

Rad took a deep breath and began to speak nervously. "I have come here tonight to speak about a subject of great personal anguish. I watch our heritage slipping away every day. Worse yet, I don't see anyone else concerned about this. What makes us who we are, but echoes of the past? If we forget that past, then who are we? We can't just let it go. At least I can't let it go without a fight."

Rad looked around. So far, so good. He breathed again and

continued. "I'm especially upset about the treatment of our ancestors' remains. Because we aren't nationally recognized, their bones sit in museum storehouses. This is a disgrace! We need to publicly protest this. We can't allow this disrespect anymore. Where are we putting our energy? I want to see more energy and time put into preserving our heritage and honoring our ancestors. We have to make a solid stand and settle for nothing less than all of our demands being met. If all of us unite, we will succeed."

Rad stopped for a minute and scanned the crowd. They were thoughtful, but not enthused. It was time to stop. "Thank you very much," he said flatly and sat down feeling disappointed.

The Elders conferred for several minutes. Joe felt relieved. Rad had dropped all recriminations and gotten to the point after all. The audience hadn't gone for the rabble rousing, and Rad had had the good sense not to push it. His point was good, and some people had listened to him, but their response was closer to guilt than enthusiasm.

Finally, the Elders finished conferring and looked to Soft Rain to speak. She was one of the oldest and quietest of the Elders. Joe knew they often looked to her for philosophical decisions. She was a small round woman with deep wrinkles and long grey braids.

"All of the issues always need to be considered," Soft Rain said quietly. "Where should our focus be?"

Joe felt she was very aptly named. Her beautiful voice rang gently, lulling him towards sleep.

"We, the Elders, have a difficult duty in guiding the community..."

Joe jerked himself awake, and Lilly rolled her eyes. He didn't intend to be disrespectful, but he was exhausted. Rad had spoken well. Joe hoped he would receive some recognition for it.

"Steven stressed the importance of our heritage eloquently," Soft Rain continued. "It warms my heart to hear it."

Joe held his breath, waiting for the 'but'.

"A divided focus may seem ineffective at first," Soft Rain explained. "Eventually, with conscientious, persistent attention we can make lasting changes. It does not come in a flash or a headline. Sometimes it is all but inapparent. Action after action seems to bring no response. Yet, quietly the interweaving of efforts brings progress. Sometimes unexpected opportunities arise because many small things all happen at once. Then a situation can turn around."

Rad looked downcast, and Joe felt for him. The Elders were already set on an approach, and nothing Rad could say would made any difference.

"The duty of the Elders," Soft Rain said resolutely, "is to guide the younger ones with the wisdom of our experience. Because this approach requires the perspective of the long years, we realize the younger members may not fully understand or trust it. In fact, we expect impatience, but we must continue to pursue all avenues equally and steadily."

Joe stifled another yawn.

Ellen came in, leaving the door of her apartment open. She put down her bag and threw her coat over a chair. All day she had wondered if her new sweetie was going to call her. There was a message waiting for her. Eagerly, she pressed the button to see if it was him.

"Hi, Ellen, this is Alex." Her heart raced at the sound of his voice. "Sorry I can't see you for a while. I've come down with this really awful flu bug. I'll call you when I'm feeling better. Bye."

This was devastating! She fell head over heels for this guy, and he was blowing her off after only one date. Wait! Maybe he really did have the flu. Maybe she was making too big a deal out of it. Then again she had heard this before, and it meant they did not want to see you any more. They were just saying they were sick. Then again, what was he supposed to say to her if he really was sick?

More to the point, what should she do? What could she do? She could call him back to ask if he was really sick or just making it up to avoid her. If he was telling the truth, that would alienate him. If he was lying, he would just stick to the lie. She was stuck waiting. Either she would hear from him or she would not hear from him.

The first things she did were the automatic ones. She put a frozen dinner in the oven, checked her mail, and lowered the blinds.

Ellen decided that getting back to work was the best idea. She pulled out today's prize, a copy of a will for one of the Wampanoag cases. Hopefully, it was pertinent. The name was correct, and the timing was about right. She had not had time to read the content, because the office was closing. Thankfully, they had a copy machine.

Even with her expertise, reading eighteenth century writing was difficult. It required concentration, and try as she would, she did not have it just now. If only she knew about Alex...

Caleb knew the pile was here somewhere. He had stacked up all of the annoying files to hand off to Susan. The sooner those files were off his plate, the better.

He was an archaeologist. Definitely, he was not an administrator, and he detested managerial tasks. For the most part, he totally ignored them. Some things he neglected intentionally. There were other things that he forgot about, and he just did not know what to do with the rest of them. Fortunately, Joshua had seen the light. Rather than take on the duties himself, he combined two part-time jobs and hired Susan.

Caleb felt that Joshua had chosen well. Certainly she was no administrator. That was obvious by how she carried herself. She was young and eager; that was the important part. Joshua could pile flunky work on her. Probably, she would never even think to delegate it, let alone refuse it.

Here were the files. Excellent! No more scheduling, repair logs, or procedures to bother with. As far as that problem of the inventory, he could just deny any particular knowledge. He was glad to wash his hands of that problem. He did not cause it, and he did not solve it. Thankfully, it was now someone else's problem.

Archaeology was his life's passion, and it felt good to be rid of the distractions. Reconstructing the past was discovering the real history of mankind. Left to his own devices, he would dabble in it endlessly. Nothing could possibly be more fascinating.

Caleb picked up the boxes of files. The sooner they got to Susan's desk, the better.

Susan stood checking her messages and surveying her office. She just did not know how to handle this job, and a message from Dr. Moorland asked her to leave an update on his voice mail. It was a dismal situation.

For that matter it was a dismal office. She had moved all the extraneous furniture and boxes into the corner. Now you could really see how badly the room needed fresh paint. The old peach color was flaking. The fluorescent lighting was poor, and it was all absorbed by the dark concrete floor.

The room needed incandescent lamps, oriental screens, a heavy rug, and some very large posters. Susan jotted down a list and started to feel enthused.

Now it was time to attack the actual work. She randomly unpacked some of the files from Dr. Emerson. They looked a little tattered. She appropriated a filing cabinet which was all well and good until she tried to file them.

She could not figure out what they were about. When she looked inside, they made even less sense. Most of Dr. Emerson's notations were cryptic to put it mildly. It was hard to read what the words were, and almost impossible to figure out what they meant.

It was time for a break. Susan decided to go to the rest room and get a cup of tea. As she turned the corner, she walked right into Dr. Emerson.

"There you are, Susan," Dr. Emerson said pleasantly handing her a large box. "I've been meaning to get these to your office."

"Thank you," Susan stammered taking the box without looking at it. "I was actually going to ask you about some of these things..."

"Yes, of course," Dr. Emerson said as he strode away. This

was exactly what he had been afraid would happen. He did not want to be pinned down to any of the information he was handing off to her.

The clatter of Susan's heels reverberated in the hall as she scurried to keep up.

"Dr. Emerson, there's some things I don't understand," Susan began. This was her opportunity to get some help.

"Perhaps I could talk with you another time," Dr. Emerson said briskly.

"About the files you gave me..." Susan asked breathlessly.

"Yes, that's the last box of them," Dr. Emerson replied entering his office. "You should be all set now." He closed the door behind him.

Susan stood outside feeling helpless. As much as she wanted to barge in and demand he decipher his terrible writing, she was afraid. She had a pretty good idea of what his reaction would be. Not only would he not answer her, she would probably be fired outright. At the very least, he would complain to Dr. Moorland, and she would be in some kind of trouble. In the end, she slowly walked back to her office carrying still more indecipherable files.

After the meeting, Steve got in his truck and drove home slowly. Driving in the dark relaxed him and let him think. He detoured past a long string of cornfields. There used to be so many more cornfields. Driving past superstores and warehouses just did not give you the same peace of mind.

Tonight had been a terrible disappointment. It was not unexpected, but it was still a let down. The important part was that he had tried. It had been futile and a little bit embarrassing, but he had done his duty. That was all very well, but it left him angry and agitated.

Now he had another challenge. He had to go home and see Melissa. If she saw that he felt this way, she would be up all night consoling him. That was the last thing he needed; he had a plan to execute.

Steve took another detour. First he had to get a hold of his emotions.

Melissa anxiously watched television and waited for Steve. The blue couch in the den was her favorite place. It was soft and cushy as well as beautiful. When she was situated just right, she could watch television or stare into the fireplace.

As much as she hated getting up, she jumped up to look out the windows every time she heard a noise. He would be upset. She knew he would be upset. The mood of the people just was not the way he was hoping it would be. He was going to need her to console him. With any luck at all, that would be the end of this, and he would settle down for a while.

Long ago, she had stopped going along on his capers. When he was being Rad the radical, she stayed home and waited.

What else was there to do? She loved him. Sometimes, she even agreed with him. However, she drew the line at participation. Helping him pick up the pieces took enough out of her. He was so bright and so dedicated to his causes. If only he could devote himself more moderately, he would be incredibly effective.

She wondered how he would react tonight. Usually he raged when he was disappointed. He probably come home yelling and ranting about how wrong everyone and everything was. When they were first married, she worried about it, because he seemed so upset. Then she realized he was just venting. Now she listened with one ear and threw in a consoling comment here and there.

On the other hand, he might sulk. Sometimes he did that instead. It was easier to be around him when he sulked, but his sulking fits sometimes lasted for weeks. She was not sure which she preferred. Either way, he would need some sympathy from her.

Finally, she heard his truck pull in the driveway. Through the window she watched him trudge up the walk. She pulled her fuzziest blanket over her shoulders and went to the kitchen to meet him.

"Hi, Honey," Melissa said kissing him on the cheek.

"Hi," Steve muttered. He threw his windbreaker over a chair.

"How was it?" Melissa asked as though she could not tell by looking at him.

Steve huffed a large sigh and opened the refrigerator door. "Bad," he answered without looking at her.

To Melissa, the signs were unmistakable. He was going to sulk. "Aww, Honey," she said, rubbing his back.

Steve looked up from the refrigerator to give her a quick hug. He pulled a casserole out and put it on the table to pick on. "It could have been worse. They took me seriously. They just didn't care about what I had to say."

"That's too bad."

"Nobody cares," Rad said dejectedly as he put a plate in the microwave. "That's all it comes down to. Nobody cares."

"What did they say?"

"Nothing," Rad said. "I talked. Then I sat down. No one said anything."

"What about the Elders?" Melissa asked. "They must have said something."

"They were polite. They said my concern warmed their hearts." Steve waited, but Melissa was waiting for more. "They are going to do a little of everything for a long time, and somehow all of a sudden, it's all going to work out." He tried not to sound too bitter.

"So what do you think?"

"I think I wasted my time."

"That's not true," Melissa said emphatically. "What you did was important, and I'm proud of you."

"Thanks, Miss," Steve said quietly.

"What're you going to do now?"

"Catch some TV," Rad replied. He was purposely misunderstanding her question to mislead her. There was no way he wanted her staying up with him just now.

Melissa concluded that he was sulking for sure. He had not even given her a blow by blow account. This sulk might last for months. There was no sense in sticking around for this. "I'm heading up for bed. Are you staying up late?"

"Probably." Rad took his dinner out of the microwave.

"Good night," Melissa said. She gave him a peck on the cheek.

"Good night," Rad said studying the floor. He picked at his

24

food and waited until he was sure she was in bed.

When he was sure it was all quiet, he let himself think about the meeting while he paced around the kitchen. The more he thought about the meeting, the angrier he got. Pretty soon, he was replaying the evening in his head and pacing frantically.

He should not have gone to the council meeting. All they did was ignore him, and tempt him to reveal his plan. The whole thing enraged him. He could not tolerate their indifference.

It was time. It was more than time. When he first considered the Hillman Plan, he should have executed it immediately.

Rad picked up the book and looked at it. 'Talking God' was written by Tony Hillerman. He was damn bright and insightful for a white guy. Obviously he sympathized with the Indian point of view concerning ancestors.

Rad opened the dog-eared page where the shocked museum administrator opens the box of her own ancestors' bones. He wanted them to feel the same outrage he felt at the thought of his ancestors' skeletons being held captive or irreverently displayed.

No research was needed to find out who the museum's administrator was and where his ancestors were buried. Dr. Caleb Emerson's home was featured some time ago in the Sunday newspaper. It was an old estate outside the city complete with servants' quarters, carriage house and family cemetery. The article went on at some length about the family's history.

Rad reviewed the article and breathed a huff of commitment. He typed the letters he had been composing in his head for a week. He had to let Melissa know he was going for a while, but if he told her anything specific, she would be in trouble too. He had to leave her out of it. He wrote a real explanation to Joe. It felt good to write it, but he decided not to send it, at least not yet.

Now for THE letter. This one was for Dr. Caleb Russell Emerson, the museum's administrator. First, he wrote the shocking identity of the skeletons. Then came the explanation of why he dug them up and sent them. This needed to be good. It was probably going to be in the newspaper. 'As you view your ancestor's bones, you will experience the grief and despair I feel when I enter your museum. As hurt and as angry as you are now, it is only a tiny bit of suffering compared to what you have inflicted upon us.'

Steve read it again and again. It was beautiful! He wondered what the repercussions would be. There was no way to anticipate how the law would treat him. it was better not to think too far ahead. Any price he paid later was a noble sacrifice for his people.

Then he gathered a shovel, a pick and a large crate. Some time still remained for him to gather his personal power. He was on a mission.

Susan had a terrible headache. Dr. Emerson's brush off left her in a quandary. She did not know what to do next.

Jobs were dear, and she could not afford to mess up this one. She was scared to do anything, because it might be wrong. On the other hand, she was scared to ask Dr. Moorland for help, because she did not want to appear insecure.

She took a deep breath and reviewed the files. Maybe it was her imagination, but she thought she was starting to be able to read Dr. Emerson's writing. Scheduling and personnel records actually looked easy enough even though that was the part she was dreading. The procedures needed work, but they could just be embellished upon. The climate control and building maintenance logs needed some attention, but maybe she could just continue what had been started. The budget totally confused her, but it had just been approved, so she had plenty of time.

The last thing on the list was the inventory. That file was a hopeless mess. There were several lists. They were typed, printed, and scrawled by hand. None of the lists matched, and the records of items being received or transferred were equally confusing.

In the end, the only person she could think of to go to for help was Jeannie. She could not ask the secretary for direction, but she could ask for background.

Susan gathered together a few files and all her confidence and wound her way to Jeannie's office.

Jeannie peered pensively through her glasses and then looked up over them.

"I'm surprised, dear," Jeannie said pointing to the inventory file, "that Dr. Moorland didn't fill you in on this problem."

"He barely mentioned it," Susan replied. "I got the impression that it was a very minor duty."

"Well," Jeannie evaded. "Ultimately, it is going to be very minor."

Susan thought that sounded ominous. "Could you give me the background on the problem?"

"The hand written lists," Jeannie explained while she leafed through the file. "Are mostly John's lists. He used to run the storehouse about twenty years ago. After he retired, there were a succession of other people, but none of them ever completely relisted or kept up the inventory. It looks like they lost some of John's pages. The most recent attempt was about five years ago, but then the hard drive crashed. You see they bought this experimental computer system, and it never did work quite right."

"So, how do you know what's where?"

Jeannie sighed and raised an eyebrow.

Suddenly Susan understood completely. She thanked Jeannie and made a quick exit.

This explained why Dr. Moorland was avoiding her and Dr. Emerson ran away from her. No wonder her lack of experience did not matter to anyone. How could she have gotten into this mess? Their hiring motivation was clear. Administration was not what was needed. Cataloging was what was needed. She had been thoroughly misled. What now? Quitting was out of the question; she needed the money too badly. The only practical thing to do was to try to stick it out for a year or so and then write another glossed over resume.

Eric was having a restless night. Several times bad dreams woke him up. Finally, he decided to get up and turn on all the lights in his trailer. This was the kind of time he preferred having a small space. It felt cozy and comforting. He had the place fixed up just right. Most of the furniture was used, but it was all comfortable. Everything he needed fit, and it made life easy.

He could not just go back to sleep. His conversation with Melissa troubled him. What if his brother-in-law was right?

27

What if he was guarding his ancestors' skeletons? What if inadvertently he was one of the people holding them captive?

The thought left a bad taste in his mouth. He decided to smoke a joint and think it through. Some music would help that along. He put on his favorite album, 'Fly Like An Eagle.' It relaxed him and set his mind free.

What disturbed him most was that no matter how harebrained Steve's conclusion's were, the underlying facts he quoted were usually accurate. Checking them out was another matter. Who could he ask about that? Should he ask? Should he rock the boat at work and risk being labeled untrustworthy or a troublemaker? After all, he was totally unsupervised right now. He could do anything he wanted to there.

There was nothing to stop him from searching the storehouse at night by himself. There were ways to tell what race skeletons were. He could look that up, maybe they even had a book in one of the offices.

And then what? When and if he found a Native American skeleton, then what? Should he resign? Should he stay and protest? Would either of those things help? Would anyone there care if he quit? Probably not. The only thing that would accomplish was to lose a good job and mess up his own life. Should he ignore the whole issue and figure that someday he would be in a better position to make a difference? What else could he do, walk off with them?

That was it! He would walk off with them, and why not? As far as he could tell, the place was a mess. No one looked up anything there. There was no organization or inventory that he knew about. There was so much stuff they never even looked at, they might not notice for a quite while. In fact, they would probably never notice at all.

This felt right. He could give all the ancestors he found a proper burial. Melissa and Rad would approve and let the bones rest on their property. Any bones from this area was surely one of their predecessors or at least a close relative. Who better to bury them? And then at least they were buried. If there was a price to be paid later, well how bad could it be?

Steve pulled off along the side of the road by the estate with his headlights off. This was as close as he dared to come to it. There could be dogs or alarms. It would be best to proceed boldly. He gathered his tools and set across the edge of the lawn toward the back of the estate.

Even using a dim flashlight, it was pretty easy to find the graveyard. He had forgotten that graveyards at night were creepy. Reminding himself that this was a mission, he went in.

The shadows of the gravestones loomed, and he could feel the spirits of the dead present. An unearthly howl made him jump, dropping his flashlight and shaking. He did not believe in ghosts but they still gave him the jitters. Embarrassingly he realized it was only two barn cats having a spat.

Resolutely, picking up his flashlight, he looked at the gravestones. What boring names these people had. All of the surnames were very English like West, Loring, Russell, and Emerson. There was an incredible over abundance of Elizabeths, Margarets, Henrys, and Joshuas.

There was one particular ancestor mentioned in the article. Here he was, Henry West Emerson, the famous Yankee entrepreneur and robber baron. He founded the family fortune and married Eliza Loring Emerson. Her family was prominent and literary although not nearly as wealthy.

Determinedly, Rad picked up his shovel and broke the dirt. He dug steadily for what seemed like forever. The first few feet went relatively easily. Then his hands started to blister, and his back began to ache. His arms and shoulders quickly followed suit. Even his neck was complaining when he finally took a break.

Somehow he had overlooked the fact that this project involved hours of manual labor. So much for the health club keeping you in shape. He had not hit a coffin yet, but he had gone too far to turn back. There would not be another chance. Pain had to be put aside. He had to keep digging.

At long last, Steve felt the shovel hit something solid. Frantically, he dug the last bit of dirt aside. Now he stopped short. He had to open the coffin. The thought made him queasy, but this was no time to back out.

Three times he reached down to pry open the coffin lid, but the terror stopped him. He reached for it, but his hands shook and pulled back of their own accord. It was all fine to say that this was only a wooden box with a pile of inert bones, but in a deep hole in a graveyard, touching it panicked him.

He got a hold of himself and pried the lid off. The sight of the dressed skeleton was horrifying and disgusting. He had not thought about gloves. Picking up the bones was sickening. As quickly as possible, he threw them into a box.

It seemed it should be morning, but there was not even a crack of light yet. The worst was over, he told himself as he put the box and his tools into the car. He needed to hit the highway and find a place, preferably a dark place, to use a rest room and wash his hands. Coffee would be excellent, too.

At the beginning of the business day, he would ship the box to the museum. By the time it was delivered, he would be long gone into hiding.

Ellen woke feeling exhausted. She had slept deeply, but she could have used more. The clock said eleven o'clock. It had to be wrong. How could it be that late?

She reached for a glass of water. Her throat was so dry that it hurt. Drinking water made it even worse. Her throat was very sore. Her ears ached, and her nose was stuffy. She was sick, really sick.

A cold, she concluded. She had a terrible cold. It must have effected her mind, because according to the clock, it just took her fifteen minutes to realize that.

Tea was usually helpful. She decided to get up, make tea, and take cold medicine. Then she could decide what to do next.

While water was brewing for the tea, she paced around the kitchen. Today's plan was to go to the library and check for a couple of obituaries on the Lyman family. There were death records she wanted to pull for the Wampanoag Project. Also she needed to call a cemetery in Virginia.

She poured the tea and breathed in the steam. How bad did

she feel? There were projects to do. Maybe cold pills would help. She took two of them, and sipped some tea.

For today at least, there was no sense in going anywhere. She decided to sit down and go over that will she had copied off. The first thing to do was verify the name of the deceased and the date it was filed.

Pretty soon the Wampanoag files were scattered everywhere. The particular family she was following was Loring.

Now she had to check the will. Where was it? She searched the folders. Here it was, but now what was it for? Her thoughts were all muddled. It must be the cold medicine. She felt sleepy.

Again, she tried to sort through the stacks of paper and make sense of them. It was no use. She was too groggy. Going back to bed was her only feasible option.

There was an up side to all of this that overjoyed her. She could have caught this cold from Alex. If that was so, he really was sick. He would get well, and he would call her as soon as he was. There was nothing to worry about. Happily, she crawled back under the covers.

Chapter Three

Susan felt like crying. This job was going to kill her! The new lamp she bought for her desk looked nice. Other than that, nothing was going right. It was all muddled and befuddled. She felt hopelessly incompetent.

This place was ridiculous! Over a week ago, she started working here, and she still could not find her way to her office. The more she explored the labyrinth, the worse her sense of direction got. It was embarrassing! She kept winding up in the wrong places. Should she devote her time to making a map?

This computer was going to be the bane of her existence. All the connections looked secure and matched the diagram. She installed the software just like the guys from technical support directed, but it was not working. What could she do next?

In order to procrastinate, she started to explore the storehouse. Room after room was full of shelves of artifacts. All the walls were dingy white. All the shelves and floors were grey. No wonder she could not find her way around. At random, she picked a room and started checking labels and contents with the lists.

The first box was labeled 'Iron Fragments - Albany Dig.' It did contain iron fragments. All of them were properly boxed and tagged. It also contained soil samples, glass bottles, and round metal balls. There was an envelope inside labeled 'List of Contents.' All the card inside said was 'Carter's Dig.'

Susan consulted the lists. The pencil list had two references to 'Carter's Dig' and five references about digs in Albany. The neat list in blue pen did not mention anything even close. Two of the lists in blue pen named iron fragments from Albany. Reconciling the contents of this one box could easily take all afternoon.

This was not going to work. She needed a direction and a new approach. Practically, she needed to know what was here right now. That was simple enough. She decided to go through and record the actually of each box or bin. Reorganizing the place could wait. Reconciling the lists could wait. For now, recording the inventory and its location was what mattered.

Her first move was going to be looking through every box in this section. She would record the labels and the actual contents of each box. Later on, she could come back and put numbered stickers on the boxes.

Methodically, Susan began opening boxes. The first box contained teacups, bottles, bows, and pottery shards. there were a couple of boxes labeled 'Waldrhine.' There was no clue who, where, or what Waldrhine was. All of those boxes contained rocks and soil samples. The next three unlabeled boxes had crumbly patches of weaving.

She found herself getting interested in the job. It was like opening presents. The box labeled bottles contained bottles. The label was accurate. How amazing! The next container was curious. It was labeled 'furs,' but it contained bags of seeds, insects, and dried worms.

Apparently, most of the relics were left over from projects or donated by alumni. There must have been a tax write off involved. Why else would the museum accept them, let alone keep them?

In school, they pointed out that new technology sometimes made these things valuable. New tests were being perfected all the time allowing old artifacts to be properly dated or analyzed. There was also the notion of saving everything for posterity. That was all well and good, but in her opinion, none of these particular artifacts were of any real value. Although it was highly unlikely they ever would become valuable, she tried not to be ungrateful for the job security.

Then there were four more boxes of pottery shards. They were even labeled 'pottery shards.' She was pretty comfortable with pottery shards.

The next box was labeled pottery shards. She opened it casually, then she just about jumped out of her skin. Her body reacted instantly. She dropped the lid and leaped to her feet, banging her head on the shelf above her. Reeling, she scrambled away and tried to breathe normally.

After a minute, she collected her wits and looked in the box to see exactly what terrified her. Knives and shrunken heads filled the inside. How disgusting! She refused to handle these things, even packed in plastic!

That was enough for today. In addition to the aching head, she was tired, shaking, and covered with dust. Half of the contents of the room had been recorded, and that would have to do. For that last box, she wrote down 'shrunken heads and knives.' Anyone who wanted more explanation could deal with the box themselves.

Rad stopped at the nearest self-service gas station he could find. It was a cloudy, dismal morning. The gloom make him feel anonymous. He pulled the brim of a black baseball cap low over his face to pay for the gas and use the rest room.

In the men's room, he washed his hands thoroughly. Then he washed them a couple more times. After touching a skeleton, would he ever consider them clean again?

As he dried his hands, he looked in the mirror. The baseball cap was definitely the right choice. He knew how he appeared to others. At first glance, they presumed he was dim. That was the impression being large and dark made. Usually, he resented being typecast that way, but today he was going to capitalize on it.

Slow and dull, he told himself. That is what blends in. It makes you invisible and nondescript. That is what people expect when they look at you.

He knew right where to go to send the skeleton. After all, he used to work there. Deliberately keeping the baseball cap low, he stood in line to send the package.

Steve waited very patiently, thus letting himself appear dull and slow. Important people were always in a hurry.

The guy behind the desk was a dweeb, the stuffy, superior sort who sniffed a lot. So, this was his replacement. Even from here, Steve could tell the dweeb did not know what he was doing.

It was tempting to reach over the counter and hit the right button to speed things along. Not only did he want to keep a low profile, he did not want to deal with the kind of hostility he knew would accompany that move. Steve did not want to appear resentful, so he studied his shoes.

When it was his turn, he placed the box on the counter and kept his mouth shut. Maybe he could have fun playing dumb.

"Well," the clerk said. "How do you want to send this?"

Steve waited to answer.

"When do you want it delivered by?" the clerk asked impatiently.

"Tomorrow, I guess," Steve answered.

"What's in it?" the dweeb demanded.

"I dunno." Steve did not offer any more information.

The dweeb looked annoyed. "Why are you sending it?"

"Boss said to," Steve mumbled. He was thoroughly enjoying himself.

Obviously exasperated, the clerk sighed. "Where do you work?"

Intentionally, Steve hesitated. "This week, we're at the university."

"And what do you do there?" The dweeb's annoyance gave way to sarcasm. "Dig holes?"

"Yeah," Steve replied as matter-of-factly as he could.

"So, what," the clerk said testily, "do you think might be inside? Rocks?"

"Yeah, probably," Steve agreed. "Dirt too."

"Fine, we'll say dirt," the clerk snapped, noticing the queue forming behind Steve. Hurriedly, he clicked information into the machine.

Steve signed, paid, and left. He managed not to laugh until he was around the corner.

Next, he went to a fast food place for coffee and breakfast. Having been up all night, nothing really agreed with him. It was a good opportunity to discard the baseball cap and change clothes.

It was a good thing he had ordered the large coffee. Fatigue was starting to set in. He had not anticipated this, but he should have. Of course he was tired, he had not slept last night. His adrenaline level had dropped, and his muscles were stiffening up, especially his lower back. His clothes were pretty well brushed off, but the dried dirt and sweat were uncomfortable.

In just a few hours, he told himself getting back into his truck, he could have a shower and go to bed. He debated for a minute. Then he dropped his letter to Joe in the mail.

Eric waited until everyone left, and the museum storehouse was empty. Then he drank a cup of coffee and ate a few cookies while he thought. Making the decision to look for the skeletons was easy enough, but the storage areas were vast. He could easily spend the entire weekend looking for them without success. Of course, he could spend a lot more time than that looking for skeletons, because they might not be here.

The only real question was where to start looking. If you were storing skeletons, where would you put them? Somewhere, there must be a list or a directory, but searching for it was probably just as time consuming as searching for the skeletons. Then, there was luck to consider. Doubtlessly there was some pattern to the storage areas. Maybe, if you found one skeleton, you found them all.

He decided to pick a corner randomly and see what the arrangement was. The first room he picked was the one closest to his desk. It was actually a hallway, but it was full of metal shelves. There was just enough room to get through. Each metal shelf held boxes of varying sizes. Most of the boxes were cryptically labeled on the outside.

There was no consistency. Some labels were old, and some were new. Some were only numbers of letters. Some had titles of project, people's names, or locations. As luck would have it, one of the large boxes was labeled 'bones.'

Eric opened it and frowned. There were animal bones, but there were also rocks, arrowheads and pottery shards. There was a list inside. It said "bones etc." on it. There was a semi-legible scrawl about a field. That was probably a location.

The next box was labeled '#471 More Stuff.' What a strange label? The researchers must have been tired. It contained some nondescript pottery and some wooden tools. The list inside said "Marcab's Thesis."

The box labeled 'Fishhooks,' contained stuffed bats. One box was labeled 'Pots - Tiller's Dig.' It actually contained pots, how weird. He shook the next box, labeled 'Ironworks.' It sounded like it contained pottery shards, because it did contain pottery shards. There were no iron fragments whatsoever.

By the time he finished checking the entire shelf, it was obvious there was little or no organization, and the labels were not to be trusted. He suspected that the numbers indicated locations or digs, but they were still meaningless.

Eric took a break to eat his dinner and let the dust settle. He checked the environmental controls he was supposed to be watching diligently. Of course, the controls were fine. They were always fine. The humidity was always thirty percent, and the temperature was always seventy degrees. Where could you get an easier job?

He decided to try a random approach. He picked a different room and opened a box containing chipped rocks. The next one held fish bones although it was labeled 'weavings.'

Already, he was getting tired of this, but he was also too curious to stop. He opened box after box of pottery, rocks, bone tools, arrowheads, stuffed animals, dolls, insects, and horse shoes. There was some cool stuff here!

Then he found the shrunken heads. In a bizarre way, he liked them, but at the same time, he was repulsed by them. It was a much worse way to end up than being a skeleton in a box.

The decorative knives in the same box were awesome. He seriously considered taking a couple of them, but he decided to remain as honest as possible.

Just as he was about to give up for the night, he had the urge to open one last box. The label said 'lot 71.' Inside it contained a skeleton. He looked on with reverence and a little horror. Who was it?

There was a list inside, but it took him several tries to reach in and pick it up. His hand shook a little as he read 'DONATION - Skeleton - Native female - elderly - with burial artifacts originally found near Cape.'

Here he stood, looking at this skeleton. This woman was probably one of his ancestors. She was definitely a relative of some sort. Why was she in a box in a museum storehouse? She should be properly buried in a grave. He had to admit it, Rad was right on the money. This was heart wrenching.

The artifacts mentioned in the list were probably sentimental personal possessions. How could you separate those from her remains? That in itself was rotten and insensitive.

He felt like crying, but suddenly he became aware of his surroundings. It was the middle of the night, and he was at work. Room after room of shelves of artifacts surrounded him. All of them used to belong to someone. Tonight there was nothing to be done about it.

It took him a minute to put her back. He felt the need to say something to her, but he did not know quite what to say. In the end, he silently promised that he would be back.

Joe organized his desk and his thoughts simultaneously. Today was his first morning without coffee, and it was going very well. On the other hand, it was amazing what sleeping a whole night could do.

The upshot of the last meeting was to continue business as usual. Rad had made him especially aware of the issue of heritage. There was no word from Ellen about her research. The only other thing he could think of to do at the moment was to send another letter to the administrator of the local museum requesting the release of their ancestors' skeletons.

He pulled out the file. It had been almost a year since the last letter. Every year he sent the same letter without fail to the same person. Apparently, every year the same person ignored him. Still, he would call to make sure Joshua Moorland was still in charge there. This year he would rewrite the letter before he sent it again.

At first, Caleb did not even notice. He walked into his office just like he always did. As usual, he tossed the mail on his desk. When the mail fell on the floor, he noticed that there was a huge box monopolizing the entire surface of his desk. Why was there a package there? He stared briefly, trying to reconcile this new piece of information.

Peculiar, he was not expecting anything. Ignoring the scattered mail, he set about opening the box. It contained a skeleton. That still did not help him. He simply was not expecting a skeleton from anyone today.

Mystified, he opened the accompanying letter. 'These are the bones of your great-great-grandfather, Henry West Emerson, taken from your very own backyard...'

How could it be? Was it really Henry West Emerson? Henry West Emerson was his most distinguished and prominent relative.

Who could verify it? He remembered it was the maid's regular day. Caleb picked up the phone.

"Hello, Emerson residence," the maid said speaking clearly and cordially. There was only the slightest trill to her r's. "May I help you?"

"Lucinda, this is Dr. Emerson," Caleb said briskly.

"Si, Dr. Emerson. How are you?"

"Is there a large hole in the Burying Ground?" Caleb asked.

"Aaah?" Lucinda wondered if she understood him properly. Why would there be holes in the cemetery? "A hole?"

"Yes, Lucinda," Caleb spoke distractedly rummaging through the bones. "There may be a large hole dug in the Burying Ground. Please, go outside and look for me."

"Si, Dr. Emerson." Lucinda set down the phone.

Caleb picked up the skull. If he remembered correctly, this great-great-grandfather was thrown off a horse and died shortly afterwards. Curiously, the cranium was totally intact. On the other hand, there was a badly fractured femur, and a stroke would be indistinguishable from a concussion. This was a fascinating development!

"Dios mia, Dr. Emerson!" Lucinda was so shaken by her discovery that her English regressed. "Is a terrible hole. You know this?"

"Yes, I expected a hole, Lucinda..."

"What has happen?" she gasped, hoping there would be a nicer explanation than the one she suspected.

"Well, it's obvious isn't it?" Caleb explained. In the box he found the other half of the femur and held the two halves together. "Somebody dug up a body."

Lucinda shrieked. It was as horrifying as she expected. "You want me call police, Dr. Emerson?"

"No, no, don't do that," Caleb admonished. "It's nothing to worry about. I have the remains."

"Is horrible!" Lucinda cried. "I think I faint."

"Now, Lucinda, don't faint," Caleb said calmly. "There's nothing to get upset about. Just go back to work."

"Si, Dr. Emerson." Lucinda sat down slowly as she hung up. She was still in shock. A body was gone from their very backyard! This was ghastly, and Dr. Emerson was not even perturbed. Maybe she should quit and find a new job.

Caleb hung up and reflected on the bones before him. So these really were Henry West Emerson's bones. He examined the intact femur to estimate height. Somehow he had always imagined his great-great-grandfather Emerson to be a taller man. While it was here, he could just measure the skeleton. Maybe he should take a plaster cast.

Skeletons told as much about life circumstances as they did about death. He would have to examine it very carefully. Naturally, his family had been part of the upper class, even back then. Still he was curious about the nutrition and muscular development. Being upper class generally mean that you ate that much better and had a cushier life. Was that also so for his own family? What about compared to the upper classes now? Surely he could grind up just a little bit of bone to analyze.

It would be fascinating to compare the skeleton's DNA to his DNA. He could get Taylor to do that for him. Taylor might even appreciate the quality control aspect of that request. Being a direct descendant, they should share one sixteenth of their DNA. Maybe there would be some hair or dried blood they could use.

Another exciting thought crossed his mind. This would be a fine specimen to use to test Foster's new dating system, because he knew the exact date and circumstances of death.

Delighted with his new project, Dr. Caleb Russell Emerson hurried out the door to make arrangements with his colleagues.

The mostly unread letter lay scattered on the floor with the rest of his papers.

Melissa read Steve's letter when she got home. Then, fighting panic, she reread it. Whatever Rad was into, it could be serious trouble this time. She had a sinking feeling in the pit of her stomach that wouldn't go away. Looking for more meaning, she reread the letter again.

'I have to take off at least for a while until things cool down. Keep quiet and don't look for me! No matter what happens, Melissa, you know I'll find you. I can't tell you what I've done, because then you'll be implicated. Understand, I couldn't just sit back anymore and let our heritage fade away.'

Melissa sighed and blinked back tears. Where did this leave her? She was supposed to just sit and worry until Steve felt like showing up again. Great, what about jobs and bills?

As she picked up the phone to call Eric, he came in the door. Melissa ran over and hugged him.

"Eric, I don't know what to do," she cried. "Steve is gone."

Eric hugged her. "What do you mean - gone?" he asked.

"Eric, he's gone!" Melissa sobbed. "He left a vague note. All it said was that he was leaving for a while because he'd done something and needed to hide out."

"Take it easy, Sis," Eric consoled. "Did he say what or where?"

Melissa handed him the letter. "Here, read for yourself."

Eric skimmed the note. This truly sounded bad. He was worried but decided to keep it a secret. He couldn't let on to Melissa. She was almost frantic right now.

"Is this all he said?"

"Yes," Melissa said. "That's what worries me most. Who knows what he might have done?"

"Have the police or the FBI shown up?" Eric asked.

Melissa's stomach plummeted again. "No," she replied in a little voice, "at least, not yet."

"Good," Eric realized he had made her feel worse. "If they haven't shown up by now, then it's probably nothing at all. You know how dramatic Steve is."

His comfort attempt did not seem to help. Eric though for a minute. "You know Sis, he might just need some space."

"You think so?" Melissa sniffled. Any alternative sounded good to her.

"Well, yeah, he's done that before hasn't he?"

"True enough," she admitted. "But usually he picks a fight first. Then he storms out."

"So, he couldn't get you to fight with him this time," Eric shrugged. "From what you said the other day, it sounds like he sure tried hard enough."

"I just don't understand him." Melissa tried to stop crying.

"Nobody understands him, but everything is going to be fine." Eric gave her one last hug and let her go. "You'll see. Bet you anything he just needed go fishing up at his camp in Maine for a week or two. Pretty soon his head will settle down and he'll come waltzing back as if nothing happened."

"Are you sure?" Melissa asked, but she wanted to believe Eric. He was always so calm. "It's a pretty dramatic note."

"Still, the way I see it," Eric explained. "It doesn't matter, because you can't do anything anyways. Even if he is in trouble, it's not like you can help him any."

"That's easy for you to say," Melissa could not accept his reasoning. "What if Astrid were missing?"

"Sis," Eric reminded her. "Astrid kind of is missing. I hate it, but I'm giving her some space."

Why was he always right? That really exasperated her. "Okay, Eric, that's true," she admitted. "The problem is that I don't really think this is about space, although I wish it were. I think he's done something defiant and rebellious, and he's in trouble with the law."

Eric decided to try another tack. "You know, it would serve him right if you didn't worry at all. He's done this so many times that I'm surprised you take him seriously. Wouldn't that fix him, if you didn't even notice he was gone?"

"Eric, I know you mean well..."

"Not working, huh?"

"I can't just forget he's gone."

"How about if I stay over and keep you company tonight?" Eric offered. "Would that help? We'll get a movie and make some popcorn. Who knows? Rad might be home by morning."

"Do you really think so?" she asked skeptically.

"Uuummm... No, but it's possible, isn't it?"

Melissa sighed. "Staying over is a good idea. I feel so upset..."

"Can you miss him that much already?" Eric demanded playfully.

"Yes," Melissa insisted. "And who's going to pay the bills?"

"Spoken like a loving wife if I ever heard one," Eric laughed. "Should I expect you to ask for a loan?"

"Yes, you absolutely should. I'm sure he'll get fired for this."

"No problem, besides I have to ask you a small favor."

"What?"

"Let's have a cup of coffee and talk," Eric suggested.

They heated some water and settled themselves at the kitchen table with a box of cookies. The coziness seemed to comfort Melissa. Eric approached the new subject tentatively.

"It's about those skeletons - the ones Rad thought the museum had."

"What about them?"

"He's right." Eric looked her in the eye. "I looked around last night and found one of them."

"What are you going to do?" Melissa asked. "You're not going to quit are you?

"Far from it," Eric told her seriously. "I'm taking them and putting them where they belong."

"What???" Melissa jumped and spilled her coffee. "Eric, you can't do that!"

"Yes, I can," Eric said calmly, "and what's more, I should."

"You can't steal them," she objected.

"Steal? Who's stealing?" Eric questioned. "Those skeletons don't belong to the museum. If they belong to anyone, they belong to us."

"You'll get caught," Melissa protested weakly. She couldn't stand it. How could this be happening? Both her brother and her husband would end up in jail. Her mind whirled, and she imagined them sharing a cell.

"Caught by whom?" Eric continued oblivious to Melissa's shock. "I'm the night watchman remember. What am I going to do? Turn myself in?"

"Eric, they'll notice them missing," Melissa pointed out. "It's not worth going to prison."

"First of all," he said firmly. "I'm not sure about that. I didn't think it would matter much. When I found that first skeleton and looked at it, all that I could think was that this might be my own great-grandmother. The thought actually made me want to cry. Rad is right. We can't stand for this."

"Secondly, they won't notice," Eric insisted. "The whole place is totally disorganized. There is so much stuff there that taking these skeletons is like someone breaking into your house and stealing all of the paper bags. If you don't know, you won't care."

"But, what are you going to do with them?"

"Bury them," he answered solemnly.

"Where?" Melissa asked suspiciously.

"Your field, way in the back by the woods."

"MY field!" Melissa spilled her coffee again. "Why my field?"

"Because it's nice scenery," Eric offered. "Because I don't have one. And because yours is also Rad's. I'm sure he'll approve."

"Eric, I don't know..." Melissa hesitated. She agreed with the spirit of the matter. This was a good idea in theory, but the actuality of it scared her. "What if someone finds them?"

"So what if they do?" Eric asked impartially. "I'll take the tags off. They're just old bones. Who's to say that these people didn't die here?"

"Well, I guess that's true enough," Melissa conceded. This idea was starting to sound reasonable. "How many are there?"

"I'm not sure. Did Rad ever mention a number?"

"Yes, he kept mumbling about eight ancestors being held hostage at the museum."

"That's not so many," Eric said convincingly. "Besides

without Rad around, it'll give you something to do."

"What do you mean?"

"Well, there's the eight holes to dig..."

"Dig?" Melissa cried. "You want me to dig the holes?"

"They don't have to be deep holes. I'll help, but remember, I'll be arriving in the morning after work."

"I'm not digging more than one hole at a time," Melissa told him sternly. "A fine way to keep my mind off of Rad..."

"There's also the ceremonial part," Eric pointed out enthusiastically. "We have to plan that."

"That's right," Melissa agreed. "I'm sure I can come up with something appropriate."

"We have to..." Eric urged. "After all Melissa, this is our family we're talking about."

"We could burn an offering," Melissa suggested. Plans began to blossom in her mind. "And we'll sing prayers to the Great Spirit to set their souls at peace. I'm getting some great ideas about this..."

"Good, now where's the popcorn?"

Ellen felt better, not perfect, but better. Today she just had to give it another try. The best place to start was with the Wampanoag File, since it was still spread out on the floor.

It had been a few days since she had worked with it. She had to retrace her steps to refresh her memory. Here were the 'master documents,' the pay records from the Governor's office.

The aide she had made progress with was Loring. She had a sub-file for him. There was a pretty clear trail of wills and Baptismal records for several generations.

Typically, they kept leaving everything to the oldest son. Usually they specified that the mother be cared for and have certain property of her own. Frequently there was a buyout clause for siblings. This particular family, as a rule was not very prolific. The oldest son was usually the only son and frequently the only child. Then came this most recent generation, born between 1800 and 1830. There were eleven children, each of them remembered in their father's will.

Thomas Graham Loring must have been an individualist with advanced or eccentric ideas. All of his property was first left to his wife. In the event she predeceased him, all of the real property was to be sold. The proceeds were to be divided between all eleven children evenly. He specified how the household was to be divided up.

This was the exciting part. Elizabeth Loring was apparently the youngest. Some money was left to pay for her education. She additionally inherited a writing desk, her favorite team of horses, and 'Injun beadwork.'

Ellen felt like jumping up and down with glee! This was spectacular! He specifically mentioned Indian beadwork! It was not proof, but it was an incredible find.

The next step was to follow Elizabeth Loring. Did she marry? Probably she did, and hopefully either the church or the historical society would have some record. Maybe there was even a set of City Directories around to help her nail down the year.

Ellen picked up her coat. She was a woman with a mission!

Chapter Four

As soon as he pulled in, Steve knew he had made the right decision. Going to Canada was his original plan, but he was glad he had decided on Maine instead. Just thinking of the last time he went to Canada made him mad all over again.

He had taken an early morning flight into Montreal, because he got a good deal on the ticket. When he got to Canadian Customs, he was still half asleep. There was a problem with his identification; they said his passport was expired.

At first he thought they might be right. He had an old passport, and the covers looked alike. If he had not been feeling hazy right then, he would have realized what was really going on.

They put him in a special room and an official came in to talk to him. He did not catch the guy's title, but he was wearing a suit. All that mattered was the suit.

The Suit was very interested in who he knew in Canada. What, besides cheap airfare, made him choose to go to Canada? Did he have friends or relatives here? Was he sure, absolutely sure that he did not have any friends here? Again, why was he here? Where was he staying?

For once in his life, Steve did not turn into his radical self. He answered the questions politely, and suddenly his passport was not expired after all. What a coincidence?

It all left a bad taste in his mouth. It could have been a random thing, but he doubted it. He was sure they hassled him, because he was a Native American. Obviously, there was no problem with his passport.

In theory, all Native Americans are allowed to cross the borders freely, because frequently borders divided a tribe. So much for that theory. It was a bitter realization that to visit his own people on his own traditional lands, he needed the approval of the Suit.

As he drove down the trail, he put thoughts of Canada aside and surveyed the camp. Admittedly, it was not much of a camp, but he was proud of it. When he bought it, all the trails were grown over. The cabin was a burned out frame; only the foundation was salvageable. He did almost all of the work by himself.

The plot of land was a generous size. It was surrounded by woods near a small lake. The lake was probably actually a pond, but it had good fishing. It was a great place to generally commune with nature.

The cabin had a fireplace and a tin roof. The walls were roughhewn wood. There were rudimentary kitchen and bathroom facilities. He kept it well stocked with blankets and food for occasions like this.

He had not been here since his drinking days. There might even be a bottle or two stashed under the couch. He had better check and pour them out right now. This was no time to let his guard down.

Ellen began at the Presbyterian Church. They were wonderful about letting her look through their old records. This time, though, she did not have any luck. There was no Elizabeth Loring in their marriage or death records. She checked as many years as were reasonable. Unless she lived to be a hundred and ten, she was not buried at this church. She was not married here either.

Next, Ellen tried the courthouse. Unfortunately, Elizabeth was not married within the state. What to do next? Ellen sat down and considered the matter over a strong cup of tea. The last solid date she had was the date the will was filed. The local newspaper might have an article about the deceased. It was worth a try.

It was a rainy evening now, and the library was crowded. It irked her not to be able to use her favorite carrel. This one was adequate, but she preferred being next to the radiator. She requested a likely newspaper from the area, and loaded the film into the reel.

The newspapers were different back then. For your birth, death, or marriage to get into the paper, you had to be a somebody. If you were a somebody, there was no aspect of your life too trivial to mention. Card parties and picnics were frequently mentioned in the papers. On the other hand, if you were not a somebody, you were a nobody, and you passed your whole life without so much as a one line death notice.

The Lorings, Ellen told herself as she began to scan the film, were probably somebodys. They were originally from England; that always helped.

She whirled the handle forward and overshot the date by a week. Slowly, she backed up the film. It was always so tempting to stop and read the headlines. Then she usually read the articles too. It was an easy way to spend hours. Perspective made the news more interesting.

A name caught her eye, and she stopped the film. "Engagement Announcement Delayed," the headline read. "Due to the untimely death of her father, Miss Eliza Loring has changed her plans. Her father, Thomas Graham Loring, died of a sudden illness last week. He was the author of several controversial political essays as well as four historical books. At the Autumn Ball, she and Mr. Henry West Emerson were going to formally announce their betrothal. As she expects to be mourning her beloved father, she has decided to delay the announcement indefinitely. Mr. Henry West Emerson, a local successful entrepreneur proposed last month. The couple plans to wed and honeymoon at romantic Niagara Falls."

Ellen giggled to herself. So much for keeping that a secret! Then she realized that letting everyone know was the idea. This was great! Now she had a surname to check in the following Census record.

Out of interest, she checked on Thomas Graham Loring's death. It hit the front page! That was very impressive. It must have been a very literary family. Almost everyone, including Elizabeth, had at least an essay to their credit. She made a note to check for articles in 'Who's Who' types of books at the historical society.

Fascinating, it was absolutely fascinating. Dr. Caleb Russell Emerson scanned the test results and stopped to reflect on them.

He settled in the glow of his study. The room was elegant, but hopelessly cluttered. As much as possible, he kept the windows open to allow the night air to drift in. Every space held either a unique relic from his many excavations or a piece of opulent furniture. Most of the furniture was inherited. He might not have picked it out, but he would never part with any of it.

Leaning back in his favorite chair, he poured a bit more cognac into his snifter. Carefully, he reviewed each page, put them in order, and reviewed them again.

He stared off into space allowing the picture to form in his mind. The estimated height of the body was five feet and seven inches. That was not the height he had always imagined, but it was a fair height for the time. He imagined spare, dignified facial features, yet the skull indicated just the opposite. The man's face must have been round and almost jovial. Judging from the muscle insertions in the bones, there was every indication that he had done a fair amount of manual labor. Analysis of some ground bone indicated that nutrition was suprisingly good. The DNA report was right on the money, although it made him wonder where some of his other gene patterns had come from.

The other DNA patterns... He wondered which gene bands he had inherited from his great-great-grandmother Eliza Loring Emerson. The Lorings were the literary branch of the family tree. There was a complete collection of their works in the library. Much of it was political, but the historical works had made them socially prominent.

Eliza herself had penned a ladies' booklet on practical housewifery. He had always pictured her as dark and stern too. Not only that, he had no idea what she had died from...

His curiosity was piqued. How he would love to do a comparative study of his relatives' attributes and genes. Of course, it was incredibly tempting to do so, since most of them were buried in the backyard...

What a shame, it was against the law to dig them up. Any charge of unauthorized exhumation would be both embarrassing and inexcusable at his level. On the other hand, who would know? It was his house, although actually, it was still his mother's estate. He stood to inherit it, and she lived in Florida. So, who else cared?

On an impulse, Caleb fetched his spade and his lantern. Exuberantly, he walked out to the graveyard. It was easy to locate the grave, because it was the one next to the existing hole. Without further ado, he began to dig. If there is one thing an archaeologist can do, it's dig and dig quickly. While he worked, he mentally tallied up more tests to run. After all, this was a rare opportunity. He wanted to capitalize on it as much as possible.

Eric felt incredibly self-conscious at work. He sat down at his desk with his books just like he always did, but inside, he was bursting with excitement and anxiety. Tonight was it! The first ancestor was going home just as soon as everyone else here went home.

The harder he tried to relax, the more jittery he felt. Every time someone talked to him, he jumped. Then he remembered that he could always change his mind and not take anything at all. That thought carried him through until the time when everyone else left.

When they were finally gone, he sat at his post as though he were paralyzed. This was it! All the nervousness flooded back while he waited. He had to make sure the coast was clear. Everyone had to be out of the building for the night. If one of them forgot something and came back at the wrong time, he was done for, and none of the ancestors would be rescued.

About an hour elapsed before Eric finally made his first move. He went to the room with the skeleton in it and checked the box. It was still there. Of course it was still there, he told himself. Where would it go? His nerves were really doing a job on him.

Keeping just out of camera range, he carried the box out to the lobby. He turned off the alarm and the camera and walked outside with the box. With his heart racing, he put it into the back of his truck under a tarp. Then he strolled back inside.

He was done! A relative was rescued! If anyone questioned the alarm record, he could just say that he forgot his coffee, or his book, or his dinner. This was easy! It was also exhilarating! Still, he was relieved to have it over with.

He checked the time. It was only midnight; he still had seven hours to go. This was going to be a long night of waiting. Then it occurred to him that he should move some boxes onto the shelf where his ancestor had been, so that there was not an obvious gap where a box was missing. Not only that, he should keep searching for more ancestors.

Continuing the mission made him feel better. It helped the adrenaline rush wear off. He found two more ancestors, but he decided to wait until next week for Melissa's sake. Solemnly, he promised them a rescue and a proper burial. He set their boxes aside in another more sparse room and kept looking for more skeletons.

By morning, Eric was exhausted. The morning guard arrived late in his usual comatose state. Eric just yawned and waved as he left.

As casually as he could, Eric walked out of the building and drove away. As soon as he was out of sight, the excitement hit him again. He wanted to yell and floor it in high spirits, but knew that was a stupid thing to do. He could not risk getting pulled over by a cop. Sadly, he refrained and headed to Melissa's place, carefully keeping within the speed limit.

Joe liked a neat desk. He never had a neat desk, but he tried. Lilly usually tossed notes, copies, mail, and supplies wherever she thought they would catch his attention.

Sometimes, she came up with some unique locations. Vitally important messages were usually hung from the light cord. Reasonably urgent business messages were propped in front of his computer screen. Regular messages were just scattered on his desk. Occasionally she folded these into origami animals. It was an unorthodox system, but it worked very well.

Today the desk was worse than usual. This was his penance for leaving early the other night. First he surveyed the light cord messages, and cursed himself for coming in late today. He took the monthly supplies of pens, toilet paper, tea bags, and paper towels off of his chair and on to the floor.

Finally, he brewed a cup of tea and corralled the paper animals and sorted through their messages. None was remarkable or urgent, but there was a message from Ellen. Today was their meeting day, and she was due momentarily.

As he cleared off his desk, she arrived with a hefty stack of papers. After the usual chatter and tea making, they got down to business.

"This," Ellen said proudly waving a stack of papers, "is what I've discovered." Beaming, she handed him the papers.

Joe looked them over slowly. They appeared to be a rather lengthy Will, a list of household effects, and burial expenses to be reconciled.

"I started," Ellen explained, "with the records from the Governor's Office at the time of the missing Wampum Belts. It took a lot of searching, but as you remember, I got them, even the payroll and daily logs. Those things tell me who was who back then."

"Yes, I remember that," Joe confirmed.

"I started tracing the higher officials, as they would be more likely to have access to spoils of war and that sort of thing."

"So what do we have here?" Joe asked while he scanned.

"I'm tracing all of the officials simultaneously. One of them was a Loring."

"Shouldn't you trace one official at a time?"

"Not if you want me to finish within our lifetime," she told him sternly. "It just doesn't work that way. Anyway, all of Jo Loring's effects went to his widow - a rather young widow by the way and unusual for that era. Usually, it all went to the first son with financial provisions for the wife."

Joe nodded her on.

"She had three children, but she disinherited all of them, except for the youngest," Ellen explained excitedly. "He got everything. He only had one surviving child, a son, who naturally got everything. That child left everything to his oldest grandson, since his son, again the only child, predeceased him. The grandson had two children; everything went to the son. That son had eleven children. He left each of them something, and that is the will you're looking at."

"No wonder it's lengthy," Joe commented.

"The salient part here is right here," Ellen pointed, "Elizabeth Loring, the youngest child and favorite daughter, is left Indian beadwork along with her two favorite horses and a writing desk. Isn't that exciting?" Ellen stood back beaming with delight.

"So," Joe said slowly, trying to take it all in. "You think the beadwork might be the Wampum Belts?"

"I certainly think there's a strong possibility," Ellen said enthusiastically. Surely he was going to make the same connection she had. "There was no mention for a couple of generations, but you wouldn't mention a stolen item until it had been forgotten about. Also if she was the favorite, wouldn't you leave her something of value if not money?"

"I guess I couldn't say..." Joe began carefully.

Ellen almost snatched the documents away. Whether it was evident to him or not, she was thrilled with her find. "It's the first mention of anything Indian.. uh... Native American. I want to go with it."

"Yes, by all means," Joe agreed. "Definitely continue."

"Alright." Ellen spoke calmly, but inside she was offended. This was a very promising discovery, and the least he could do was acknowledge that. She saw no reason to tell him that she had any more information at this time. "Then I'll be on my way."

Joe politely walked her to the door. Then he sat down to look over the items in the will. Horses, livestock, tools, chairs, land, dishes...

The question was could this mention of Indian relics and beads be the missing Wampum Belts. He did not want to risk getting his hopes up in case it was a wild goose chase. It would mean so much to get the history of the people back, but what if they were disappointed? There was not much to do except set it aside for a while and see what else turned up.

Stoically, Susan arrived at the museum. She would make a success out of this yet. All she had to do was to keep on trying.

Right?

Then her pager went off. Jeannie gave her a pager, because everyone else had one. Susan had no idea why she needed a pager. It was hard for her to imagine a storage emergency. But, now the pager had gone off, and she had no idea what to do. Just finding her way through the labyrinth to her office was still a challenge. Her telephone yielded no clues. Finally, in her desk, she found the pager manual and directory. Those would need to be read too. She called in and found that her sister had called. They were meeting for lunch.

She looked over the volume of her work load. It was actually very manageable unless you included cataloging the entire collection. If you want to be the manager, you have to manage. That is what they taught her in school. She decided to devote the mornings to her actual managerial and administrative duties. After a late lunch, she could spend an hour or two a day sorting every single piece in the storehouse and slowly but surely make some progress.

With this schedule in mind, she spent the morning learning about the security systems. There were cameras at every door. The humidity was kept at thirty per cent, and the temperature was held at exactly seventy degrees Fahrenheit. There were humidity and temperature sensors in every room. Any variation caused an alarm and a blip on a circular graph. The graph mystified her, but understanding it could wait. It was time for lunch with her sister.

Melissa saw Eric's truck pull in. She wanted to strangle him. How did he talk her into trying to dig a stupid hole anyways? He better have a skeleton with him, and it better be one of her ancestors. Her back was already killing her.

She heard him whoop as he bounded up her walk.

"Hey, Sis, I'm here!"

"I know," Melissa answered dryly. "And so does the rest of the neighborhood."

Eric scooped her up in a big hug. "I just couldn't hold it in anymore."

"I can't... " she started to object, but his delight melted all her annoyance. "I can't believe we're really doing this."

"Believe it, Sis," he told her exuberantly. "Believe it and revel in it. Ours is a glorious mission."

"Glorious mission! Are you high?" Melissa demanded half seriously.

"Ever since I carried that box out the door," Eric said emphatically. "I've been like this. It's great! Is everything ready? Come on!" He pulled her out the door.

They drove behind the house and through the woods. Eric jumped out of the truck and waved Melissa around to the back. Silently, he opened the box and waited while she looked inside at the bones.

At first, she recoiled. There was an element of horror at seeing a body without a soul. Then a heavy feeling of sorrow and grief swept over her. She allowed herself to be engulfed in it like a swimmer overcome by a wave. It was unexpected and compelling. All the despair and humiliation of her people's collective past cried out to her from this one offense.

Eric waved a tissue in front of her face. "I thought you would need this," he whispered.

"You were right. It's so awful..." Melissa started but could not continue.

"Come on," Eric said taking the box out of the truck. "Let's do something about it."

Melissa recovered herself. "Here's the hole. I hope it's deep enough."

"Yeah," Eric said taking the tags off the bones. "It looks fine."

"I went to visit Auntie Mae," Melissa said.

"How is she?" Eric asked busily.

"She's old," Melissa said guiltily. "She can hardly see. It made me feel bad that I haven't seen her in so long. She gave me some sweetgrass. Originally, I thought we could just smoke some weed, but now I'm glad I brought the sweetgrass. Aunt Mae told me all about how it's our people's most sacred traditional herb. It's really much more appropriate."

"Did you get any songs?"

"Three of them - rhythms and words. She was delighted that I was asking." Melissa considered it a minute. "I'm going to go back and learn some more, too."

"How much did you ask her?"

"All I had to say was 'What were traditional funerals like?' and she talked on and on."

"You should have tape recorded it," Eric suggested as he finished taking tags off.

"I wonder if we should invite her to help us?"

Eric thought it over. "I'm not so sure that's a good idea. Mom always said never to tell her a secret. Also Auntie is very strict about breaking the law."

"That's true," Melissa admitted. "It might really upset her. We can give them a reasonably traditional funeral. There's a couple of details where we're going to have to wing it."

"That's okay, Sis," Eric said. "I'm sure she'll appreciate the effort."

"Then let's start with smudging," Melissa directed, picking up the braid of sweetgrass.

At the end of the ceremony Melissa felt different still. She could feel a glow around her. The sensation was tranquil and powerful. She could only describe it as a holy feeling. As she glanced at Eric, he seemed to glow too.

"Eric, I was mad at you about digging the hole," Melissa admitted. "Now I'm ashamed of that."

"I think you have to experience seeing the bones," Eric said solemnly. "Until I did, I thought Rad was blowing it out of proportion. Then I saw what he meant, and now I'm rescuing all of them. Are you with me?"

"All the way!" Melissa confirmed. "I can't believe I almost bailed out over a ripped fingernail and an aching back."

"Now you see why I didn't want to dig the holes," Eric said solemnly.

Melissa tried to punch him in the stomach, but he jumped out of the way with his eyes twinkling.

When Susan returned from lunch, she gave the computer a

dirty look and decided to catalog the area she had started to explore the other day. Even if she just jotted down the labels and contents of the dozen boxes there, it was a start. She could reconcile it with the other lists and then try to get the computer working.

The project started smoothly, then she realized there were two more boxes here now than there were last week. Stealing would be understandable, but who would add to a museum's collection? Obviously, she was mistaken about the location. She decided to start at another location, but the thought nagged at her.

Randomly, she picked another shelf in another room. Carefully, she recorded the labels and the actual contents. Then she went to reconcile this information with the old lists. It was boring, but it beat tangling with the computer.

Chapter Five

Ellen still had not heard from Alex. At the end of their date, he was very specific. He said he would call her. Unless he was dead, he should be over that virus by now. If he was dead, she could forgive him for not calling her. Off the top of her head, she could not think of any other acceptable excuses. What should she do?

If he was a jerk, he would never call. Yet, they had such a great time... If he was really a nice guy who was just tied up with something else, he would be glad to hear from her. Maybe he lost her number or it was some kind of test. These things happened. She debated the issue with herself for quite some time before she picked up the phone.

"Hello, Alex," she said cheerfully. "It's Ellen. How're you feeling?"

"Oh, uhh... hi," Alex stammered. "I didn't expect to hear from you."

"Well," Ellen prompted. "I thought you'd be over the flu by now."

"Yeah, I am, but, umm..." Alex squirmed.

This did not bode well. "Is something wrong?" Ellen asked directly.

"There is... It's, uh, you've caught me at a bad time," Alex hedged. "I've really got to go. I'll call you, okay. Goodbye." He hung up the phone.

"Jerk!" Ellen yelled into the dead receiver. "You are a worthless jerk, and I hate you!"

There was no sense in calling him back. She knew his type. They were spineless cowards. He was probably married or engaged or something. One romantic date and he was running away. She was glad she had not slept with him.

She was disappointed and angry. No matter how hard she tried not to let it happen, these things always hurt her feelings. In her head, she knew it was only him. He was a loser. There were a lot of men like him. They would turn on the charm until they had won you over. As soon as they saw you were falling for them, they dropped you. They could be afraid of commitment, insecure, having second thoughts, or lying to themselves. It did not matter. It was hurtful, and no matter how much you knew it was not about you, it was hard not to take it personally.

As she got older, it seemed to get worse. There had been so many hurts, and the effects seemed cumulative. Then there was the embarrassment of being misled. Maybe the pickings were just slimmer at this age. She did not know. Her heart hurt just now, and that was all that was important.

Usually, she threw herself into her work when life distressed her, but that brought up another disappointment. Her last meeting with Joe was dismal, and she was kind of miffed at him.

She thought Joe would be thrilled about the Will. Here she was, jumping up and down with joy, and he was barely even interested. In light of that, she decided to save the information about Eliza's marriage for the next meeting. What was the fun of the job, if your client was not excited too?

Ellen decided she needed to get out and have some fun with friends. First she would plan something fun and social for this evening. She would see about the census records when she good and felt like it.

Steve woke up feeling disoriented. This time he was less disoriented than the last few times he woke up, so he decided to try getting up. Sitting up promptly reminded him why he was still lying down. He was exhausted, and his whole body was screaming with pain.

Now, he remembered vividly. This was why he had gone back to bed the last three times he tried to get up. He needed aspirin and coffee desperately.

He yawned and stretched a little and headed very slowly for the kitchen. What time was it? What day was it? Where was the aspirin? He needed coffee to remember. Where was the coffee? This was really hard. Why was he in such a daze?

It had been a long time since he had been Rad the radical. He did not remember it being this tough. He had been out all night with hijacks plenty of times before. Why was it this bad? Could he be getting too old for it?

That last thought jolted him into action. No way, there was no way, he was going to accept that idea. He was not too old, and he never would be. All he needed was to get the coffee going.

The percolator was on the stove. There was nothing like a fresh perked pot. The coffee was in a jar by the canisters. There was bottled water around here somewhere. He found it next to the refrigerator and started the pot.

Running water was the one detail that he had not worked out properly. The water came from a well. He needed to prime the pump to get any water running. Originally, he planned to do that as soon as he got there. The mistake he made was lying down for just that one minute.

The shower had waited this long. The damage was done; every muscle in his body was killing him. He went to the bathroom and took a couple of aspirin. In a couple of hours, he could have a hot shower and stretch out. In the mean time, he needed to get things together.

He consulted his checklist of things to remember opening and closing the camp. Since it was still more or less the middle of summer, he could skip dealing with the furnace. The fireplace was a different matter; even in the summer, he enjoyed a fire at night.

This would be great! He could fish, relax, and enjoy the woods. He hoped it would be a few days until the FBI showed up to take him away.

Eric arrived at work feeling comfortable and relaxed. His first night smuggling out ancestors was the hardest. Now he had three under his belt, and it was easy. He had already found three more. Only two still needed to be located.

The smuggling had fallen into a routine. First he would locate the skeletons and set the boxes aside or earmark them in some way. On another night, he would simply put one of the boxes in his truck. He usually did this during the dead hours between three and five a.m. It was a good time to step outside, because it was still very dark and quiet. The bar were closed, and most jobs did not start for hours. Anyone else who was out and about at that time would not be prying into his affairs, because doubtlessly, their affairs were more nefarious.

Eric opened a book and poured his coffee. He had a couple of hours to kill before he rescued another ancestor.

For most people, three a.m. is a difficult time to get up. Dr. Caleb Russell Emerson took it in his stride. He never cared what time he slept. He was aware that it bothered other people to be put off of their routine, but it never phased him. Jet lag had little effect on him either. Sleep could be made up later. Work was what mattered.

His ancestral skeleton study was proving to be fascinating. There were two more freshly unearthed skeletons waiting to be studied. The decision to take them in to the museum at an absurdly early hour, was a practical one by his standards. He wanted to avoid questions about his own personal projects. The exhumations were technically illegal, and he realized a lot of people would have a problem with that. Also, he should not be using the museum's facilities for any research except theirs, but he felt this was one of the perks of being a professor.

Eric was standing at the door of the museum, holding a a box containing an ancestor, when he heard the vehicle pull up. He barely had time to scoot the box behind the desk and sit back casually.

Caleb saw the movement of the guard in the window of the door. He hesitated, and then he put his box of contraband down. He had forgotten all about this. In addition to the guard, there was the after-hours log book and camera security. No one knew why they were there, but there they were. He seriously doubted anyone would ever look at the video tapes, but he hesitated to be questioned, as the boxes were pretty hefty and constituted a delivery. No one would question him coming in insanely early; that would merely be considered eccentric. Coming in insanely early with packages was different. It might raise suspicion about the contents.

He needed a new approach here. What would distract that guard? Then the idea struck him.

Caleb entered and signed in with no further ado and with out his boxes of bones. He went towards his office and turned off suddenly. He picked up the sensors to the environmental alarms and blew on them long and hard. As expected, the graph jumped, and he heard a distant beeping. Caleb hurried away.

Eric was sprawled at his desk debating whether it was riskier to move his ancestor outside to the truck or back to the shelf. Then the alarm went off. That was weird. Okay, first things first, he had to go and check out the alarm problem.

Caleb made sure Eric was away from his post. He strode over to the alarm station and turned off the door alarm. Then he hurried out, grabbed the boxes and lugged them well around the corner. Then he came back and stood at the alarm panel, pretending to study it intensely.

Eric investigated the area the alarm was going off in. He returned to his post to see Dr. E. standing almost right next to his ancestor's skeleton, and his mouth went dry.

"Can I help you Dr. E?" Eric asked, trying not to let any worry show.

"Yes, you can." Dr. Emerson answered with confidence. "Eric isn't it? I left some papers in my car, and I had to go and get them. So I flipped off the alarm, and now I can't seem to see which one it is."

"Right here, Doc." Eric flipped the switch with relief. "Don't worry about it, I'll record it in the log for you."

"Thank you." Caleb exited quickly. Once around the corner he grabbed his boxes with relief.

Eric sat back and thought about what to do next. This was a pesky development. Dr. E. was not a cool guy, and this was very bad timing. If only he could be sure Dr. E. would go to his office and stay there for a few minutes. Then a thought crossed his mind, a page, if Dr. E. got a page, he would at least have to stop and check it out. He dialed Dr. E's page number and put in nonsense for the callback number.

Quickly, Eric flipped off the camera and the alarm. He hurried outside and slid the box into the back of his truck. When he returned, he breathed a sigh of relief. He would have to put off the rest of his search until tomorrow, but that was okay. For the moment, he just wanted to sit down until his heart stopped pounding.

Caleb Emerson jumped when his beeper went off. He looked at the number but did not recognize it. That did not mean it was not important. More than once a colleague had called him at this hour with an important discovery. It was impossible to keep time zones straight when you were elated over a find.

He dialed the number as it was shown and reached an out of service recording. Checking his beeper to confirm its accuracy, he redialed the number and got the same annoying recording. He got the operator to dial it. She confirmed that it was nonsense.

This was frustrating. He called the pager service.

"This is Dr. Caleb Russell Emerson, I'm having a problem with my pager."

"Yes, sir," The operator answered. "What can I help you with?"

"I just received a page," Caleb explained testily. "When I called back, the number was out of service."

"It's probably a mistake, sir," the operator said cheerfully.

"Of course it's a mistake!" Caleb snapped. "The problem is, how do I get in touch with the person who paged me. It might be important."

"Usually they call back," the operator offered.

"Well, this one hasn't!"

"They sometimes dial the wrong page number, sir," the operator said.

"You think they dialed the wrong page number and the wrong call back number?" Dr. Emerson argued. "That's ridiculous!"

"It happens, sir." The operator said, trying to placate him. "Usually, these things straighten themselves out soon enough."

"I can see this won't get me anywhere. Goodbye." Dr. Emerson snapped and hung up the telephone. It was all annoying. The call was annoying. The telephone company was annoying. The pager was annoying, and the pager company was very annoying. He decided to forget it and get on with his experiments.

After he hung up, the operator went directly to her supervisor. She had dealt with Dr. Emerson before. This was definitely a problem to tell the supervisor about.

Eric wrote some drivel on the chart and in the book about the environmental alarms going off. This was a very serious problem for him, especially because there was absolutely no reason whatsoever for that alarm to have gone off. He was supposed to write down the reason why the alarms went off on the chart and in the log book. No one had ever addressed what to do if there was no reason at all. What if it meant the entire system was malfunctioning?

Why did this have to happen on one of his smuggling nights? He was trying to avoid calling attention to himself, especially on a night when he had turned off a door alarm.

The alarms were his virtually his only real duty. All that he could do was to try to deal with the problem. He pulled out the instruction book and checked the whole system. There was nothing wrong with it, at least nothing that he could find. Smuggling or not, he had to let Susan know about it.

Why was he hesitating? There was no connection between the alarms and the ancestors. No matter how many people checked out the alarm systems, they would not find anything peculiar on the shelves. Eric pulled out a form and started explaining the problem and how he checked it out.

Jeannie received the yearly official letter of protest from the Wampanoag representative. It was usually polite and mundane, but this year was different. The letter was fiery, and it sounded like there might be some political pull to it.

She mulled over what to do about it. Obviously, since she was not empowered to make any decisions on the issue, she needed to pass it up the ladder. That was all well and good, but these political things always upset anyone she gave them to.

She definitely did not want to give it to Dr. Moorland. He would take all of his aggravation out on her. All she needed was to have to listen to him, grumping and grouching about the matter, until she got a migraine.

Dr. Emerson found them equally displeasing, but he was much easier to ignore. Unfortunately, he had already made it clear that this was no longer a part of his position with the museum. If she gave it to him now, he would probably throw a fit.

Susan was the person it should really go to, but she was too new to handle it. Dr. Moorland had already mandated that for at least the next three months everything of any importance was to go through him first. So, that was what she had to do... What a dismal thought.

Maybe she should throw the troublesome letter away instead. She considered all of the options and decided to compromise. In order to buffer herself, she put a note to Dr. Moorland on the envelope explaining that it was clearly a matter for Susan, but that per his request it was crossing his desk first.

Joe found the letter from Steve on his desk. He had an odd feeling about it, so he opened it right away. Just as he expected, it began, "Thanks for your help, but..."

Yes, Rad had decided to do things his own way. Nothing new about that.

Joe scanned the letter indifferently until Rad mentioned the

'Hillman Plan.' At first, he did not pay much attention. Then suddenly, he realized what the 'Hillman Plan' was.

Rad, the mixed-up radical, was referring to Tony Hillerman, the author of many popular books with Native American characters. In his book, "Talking God," a museum administrator receives a package containing her ancestors' skeletons. They were dug up and sent to her by a Native American activist.

Unbelievable! Totally unbelievable! How could Rad have done this! Didn't he know that book was fiction? Who did Rad do it to!

More importantly, Joe realized, this was a public relations fiasco for the tribe. What was he going to say to the press?

Then, he checked the date on the postmark and realized it should already have been a fiasco. Thankfully, something had gone wrong. Hopefully, the package was lost. That was good, it gave them a respite to collect their thoughts and plan strategy.

He had better get busy setting up a meeting with the Elders to discuss how to deal with the publicity and repercussions. With any luck at all, that package was permanently lost.

Susan did a double take. Today there was something in her 'in' box. How exciting! She read it eagerly. The night guard had a problem with the alarms.

She knew she should get on this immediately. The question was how to do that. She did not know a thing about the alarms. The guards were the ones who dealt with them. She presumed that they would simply take care of things like this. As she read the report, she realized she was in real trouble, because the guard did not know what was wrong.

Who could she turn to for help with this? She doubted that Jeannie would know anything about it. Who else would know about the alarm system?

As she looked through the alarm manual, she saw the telephone number to a service number listed. She called the company, and they offered to send out a repair person free of charge. This was great! She was saved! Someone else would come out and deal with it.

Getting someone else to deal with the alarm problem was such a relief. If only someone else would come out and set up the computer. Her nephew could probably do it in an afternoon. It was too bad she could not have him do it.

Then it struck her. She could get him to do it. Why not? He could not possibly do any worse than she had done. No one was ever concerned with what she did here. All she had to do was call Connor. He would bail her out of this.

"Connor, it's Aunt Susan. How are you?"

"Mom's not here," Connor replied.

"I called to talk to you," Susan said. Connor did not reply, so she continued. "Connor, I have a favor to ask you."

"Yeah, I already figured that," Connor said sounding bored. "What's the problem? Can't get the computer together?"

What a little smart aleck he was. "How did you know?" Susan gasped.

"I heard Mom talking to you."

"So, will you do it?"

"Maybe, I'd consider it," he said slowly. "You know, it would really be great if you'd drive me and my friends up to the amusement park for a weekend. Mom will pay for it, but I'm not old enough to drive, and she's busy with Gram."

Now she got it. This kid was going somewhere in the world. "Connor, if the computer is up and working by the weekend, I'll have plenty of time. I would be happy to drive you guys up there."

"Why don't you pick me up at lunch tomorrow?"

"That's great with me. Tell your mother I'll call you tonight, okay?"

No sooner had she hung up the phone, than it rang again.

"Susan Slater, can I help you?"

"This is Joanne at 'Paging Systems.' We got a call from Dr. Emerson the other night."

"You did?" Susan asked, wondering how this concerned her.

"He was rather upset," Joanne drawled. "He had a problem with his pager. We do our best, but these things happen."

"What happened?"

"He got a nonsense page," Joanne explained efficiently. "We

know he's very important, so we would like to give him a new pager with a new battery. We'll send it over today."

"Thank you," Susan responded automatically. "He hasn't complained to me..."

"We wanted to be sure you knew that we were doing our best," Joanne said. "Have a nice day."

"Thanks," Susan said as she hung up. It was still unclear why Joanne was calling her.

For the afternoon, Susan decided to catalog some more artifacts. She went to the shelf where she left off last week. As she tried to resume the project, she noticed that the boxes were either totally different or out of order.

She retraced her steps from last week. The room was full of rows of shelves like a library. She had started with the shelf that was right against the wall and successfully recorded the entire side. Midway through the room, she had left off. As she scanned her list, it matched up perfectly with the boxes on the shelves, right up until the last set she had recorded.

Then the trouble began. According to the list, the box following 'arrowheads' was 'Miller's Field.' Today it was 'Third Plot.' Last week, 'Third Plot' was on a lower shelf between two completely different boxes. The whole set of shelves was either scrambled or totally different.

How could this be? She could make one mistake but not that many. Four entire shelves were out of place!

She decided to open the boxes to compare the contents, too. The first one contained stone fishing hooks. Her list said it contained weavings. The second one had nutshells and small animal bones, when there should have been soil samples. The third box held the shrunken heads. That settled the matter in her mind. There could not possibly be two boxes of those creepy things. Forgetting about what was there last week, she went to the shelf where the shrunken heads were before. Sure enough, there was an empty space on that shelf next to the stuffed weasels.

The conclusion was inescapable. Someone was moving around the artifacts. Who would do that? Why would they want to? There was nothing of value here. What could they want to take?

This was probably something she should tell Joshua, but she hesitated. He was not very approachable. This could easily be written off as carelessness on her part. She needed to have better proof.

She came up with a new plan. That afternoon she counted the number of boxes and bins in the storerooms. It took all day, but she got through all of the rooms.

Damn the hot water heater! Steve threw his wrench down. What was wrong with that stupid thing? He had tried everything he knew. It needed a plumber. How could he call a plumber? He was on the lam!

Being on the lam was serious, and the first week was the most important. During the day, he stayed inside with the shades pulled tight. His car was hidden. He did not even light a fire in the fireplace until well after dusk. Calling a plumber was out of the question. He would have to make due with a cold shower or heat water on the stove.

This was part of the glamour of hiding out and roughing it. It was only for a few days or weeks of his life. He could take it, and more importantly, in the end, he would be proud of it.

Steve let his mind wander. That administrator must have received and opened the package by now. With delight, Steve imagined the scene. The arrogant, uptight, little WASP would stroll into his office, wearing the mandatory suit and bow tie.

Would he open the box or read the letter first? If he began by reading the letter, he would open the box almost immediately afterward. How would he react? Rad pictured him hovering over the box, gasping in horror. Maybe he would even scream. If he opened the box first and then read the letter, he might even faint. Rad found that image particularly gratifying.

Happily, Steve started heating water on the stove and opened another can of stew. The bathing water was going to take a long time to heat up. Of course, he had a lot of time. First, he would eat and clean up the water heater mess. Then he would clean up himself.

For the time being, he was fortunate. He could relax and enjoy listening to the wind in the trees and the green acorns hitting the tin roof. Now that he listened, an awful lot of acorns were hitting the roof...

Chapter Six

Caleb surveyed his office solemnly. What a mess! He had been neglecting it these last couple of weeks. It was full of bags and boxes of skeletons. He was so busy arranging tests and gathering results that his other business was piling up, too.

First his desk had filled up with papers. The stacks of paper quickly overflowed onto other pieces of furniture. Then they covered the boxes of bones and spilled onto the floor.

This afternoon there was a reasonably important board meeting. He might need to bring someone in here afterwards. Colleagues never seemed perturbed by a mess, but sometimes other people reacted badly. Board members were other people, and what was more, board members mattered.

He absolutely had to clean up and make this place presentable. Originally, he intended to keep all the skeletons in one of the storage areas. After all, that was the purpose of storage areas. So he needed to move them out there right away, otherwise there would not have room to clean up.

Caleb found an almost empty bin in the other room. It contained a few clamshell tools. They were found locally, a dime a dozen. He took the box to his office and put all of the papers in it on top of the tools. He set that next to his desk and neatened the pens on top of his desk.

Then he went back around the corner and down the hall to the storage closet. He brought back ten empty bins from the closet, and methodically moved the skeletons into them. By shuffling boxes and bins to other areas, he cleared off a long shelf.

Methodically, he packed his collection of skeletons from their haphazard containers into the storehouse boxes. There was just enough room on the shelf for all ten skeletons.

He broke down the old cartons and stacked them behind his filing cabinet. All that was left to do for the meeting was find a broom and sweep up the spilled dirt.

Tonight Eric's mission was a little different. He was smuggling the five empty containers back into the storehouse. They were starting to stack up at home, and he did not know what else to do with them. Plastic was not ecologically sound, so he did not want to throw them away. Certainly none of the ancestors wanted to be buried in them. The only thing to do was return them.

There were still a couple more ancestors to find, but there was no real hurry. This was a good thing, because Dr. Emerson was getting crazier and crazier. Eric never knew when the guy was coming in anymore. Sometimes he just stopped in and left a few minutes later. Dr. E. must have insomnia or something.

The minute everyone else was out of the building, Eric brought in all of the empty boxes. He took them directly to one of the sections he had finished searching. It looked like as good a place to stash them as any.

Putting them back on the shelf empty did not feel right to him. After some debate, he decided to break up some of the overfilled bins and distribute the relics to the empty boxes.

As he remembered, the box of stuffed weasels was very full, so he broke them up into two more boxes. Pottery was another good one. There were enough pots and shards around here to build another building. When he was done with that, there were still two more bins to fill. After some debate, he split up the knives and the shrunken heads. It was probably better for them to be stored in different bins anyway. He scattered the newly refilled boxes around a little bit to make the shelves look even again and called it a good night's work.

Rad paced. It was impossible to sleep. Anticipation was killing him. What was going on back home? They must have opened the package by now. The newspapers had to be covering it. It was too bad he had not thought to ask Melissa to save the articles and editorials.

He relished the idea of shock on the administrator's face when he opened that package. The rest of the staff would be horrified, too. That would be excellent! They would be scared to open packages until Christmas.

Doubtlessly the police would get in on it right away. Then the FBI would jump in and take over. They always did. With any luck at all a reporter with a nose for horror and gore would get the story on the front page. Maybe he should have tipped off the press. Then again, the FBI always seemed to get them to talk somehow. The press would get the story soon enough.

One part of him wanted to get out of this without going to jail. Then again, he was proud of his deed. Maybe he should turn himself in and make sure he got credit for it. No, there was Melissa to think about. She was so emotional, and she needed him there.

Idly, he wondered what Joe thought of his letter. Steve had a pretty good idea that Joe would have to express official disapproval. Privately, Steve was confident that Joe and any other of his people would at least understand, and most of them would cheer him on. Publicly, Joe might have to denounce it as a sick prank; the white world had to be dealt with and appeased in terms that even they could understand.

Rad was dying to know what Joe had said to the reporters. If Joe had told the police or the FBI anything about him, they would be here now. Joe must have said something to sidestep them. After all, public relations was his field.

He might just get away with this. How long should he wait for the publicity to die down? In his head, he arbitrarily targeted a month as a good amount of time. Sometimes he thought longer would be better. Other times he missed Melissa and wanted to go home sooner.

He might as well admit it. He felt guilty leaving Melissa in the lurch like this. Still, the FBI might pull in at any moment and make the decision for him. Waiting longer seemed wiser.

Susan returned from lunch with Connor. He looked at the computer and rubbed his hands together.

"Can you do it?" Susan asked.

"No problem," he said eagerly. "Let me at it."

"Go for it," she encouraged. "I'll be back."

Last night, Susan had decided the discrepancies in the storage area were just her own paranoia. She decided this would be a good time to humor it by recounting all the boxes. Following the same pattern as before, she counted room by room.

When she tallied them up, she had fourteen more boxes than before. How could there be more? And there definitely were more. Fourteen was too many to miss. This was ludicrous! As ridiculous as the thought of stealing from this storehouse was, the thought of adding to it was even weirder. What could possibly be going on here?

Connor interrupted her. "Susan! I'm done! Where are you?"

"I'm right over here." Susan waved between shelves of boxes.

"This place is cool! I'm putting it in my dungeon!"

"What?"

"Dungeons and Dragons - I'm creating a new dungeon level and a maze would be cool. Instead of boring museum stuff, I'm going to put really horrifying stuff in these boxes."

Susan laughed. He was close to the truth. She grabbed the bin with the shrunken heads in it and handed it to him. "Take a look at this one."

Connor peered inside curiously, then ripped the lid off.

Susan braced herself for the sight of the gruesome heads and gleaming knives. Instead, the box contained red flint arrowheads.

Connor looked puzzled. "I suppose I could put in magic red arrowheads that always draw blood?"

Susan recovered from her surprise. Now, she was absolutely certain that someone was moving boxes around. She was not likely to forget the location of that box.

"That's the wrong box," Susan said. She looked where the box had been and saw that her hair was still snagged on the shelf where she hit her head. It was the right place.

"What was supposed to be in it?"

"Something you'll want to see." Susan scanned the shelves, and found the right bin. "Here, try again."

Connor opened the bin. "Woowww! Cool!"

"See," Susan said happily, "you never know what you'll find

here."

"These are going in my next level for sure!" Connor exclaimed, digging through the box. "They can trade these shrunken heads for a lot of cool stuff. Maybe I'll make them amulets."

"What do you think of the knives?"

"What knives?"

Susan gathered her courage and looked in the box. The shrunken heads were as grotesque as ever, and the knives were conspicuously absent. Again, her theory was confirmed. Knives did not jump out of boxes by themselves.

She went back to the shelf and looked next to where the shrunken heads had been. After shaking a couple of boxes, she heard a clank.

"Take a look at these," she said, handing the box to Connor.

"Ohhh, yeahh!" Connor said as he admired them. "These are in for sure."

"Are you really done with the computer?" Susan asked.

"Are you still taking us to the amusement park?" Connor countered.

"I am if you're really done."

"Come on, I'll show you," Connor said hurrying ahead.

He leaned over and clicked on the keyboard for a second.

"What do you want to see first? Alarm records, games, inventory..."

"I have games?" Susan asked eagerly.

"Everyone always has games," Connor explained. "You just have to know how to look for them."

Melissa took a deep breath and held it, clearing her mind. Slowly, she let it out and focused on the rising sun. She began reciting the prayers just like Aunt May taught her, but she had to stop and look at the cheat sheet to finish. The first lines were coming more easily. Today she got further than yesterday. Tomorrow she would remember even more.

Aunt Mae was beginning to teach her the language. Learning to speak her own language felt good to her. It was comforting or maybe fulfilling. She must be making progress, because Aunt Mae invited her to tea with the other old ladies on the condition that she try not to speak any English.

Some of the old myths and customs were making her think about her own life. The one particular fact that stuck in her mind was that her people's healers were women. Traditionally, they used an extensive repertoire of herbal cures far superior to European medicine of the time.

There was a seed of an idea forming in her mind. What if she worked for an herbalist's license? It would be keeping to tradition, and certainly it was more interesting than payroll deductions.

The timing was excellent. It would keep her from worrying about her screwball husband too much. Nothing could completely stop her from worrying, but this new project might just be a calming distraction.

It was another Saturday late night. The museum storehouse should have been the quietest place in the city. Instead it was filled with anxiety.

Totally unbeknownst to each other, Eric and Dr. Emerson were playing cat and mouse again. Neither of them realized that the other one was up to anything. Each of them was too caught up in their own problems.

Eric was frustrated, because there was one ancestor ready to be rescued. Melissa was expecting him in the morning for the burial.

There were two more skeletons he needed to find. His search had become pretty methodical. The only area left to search was the part near Dr. Emerson's office. If he had only known what a pain in the neck Dr. E. was going to be, he would have started there. It was too late now. It seemed Dr. E. was constantly in here at all kinds of crazy hours, running back and forth for papers and books and cartons of stuff. It interrupted his searching and his smuggling.

The environmental alarms were another problem. They never used to go off at all - not ever. There was rarely even a deviation in temperature or humidity. Now, they went off frequently. It was always when Dr. E. was traipsing in and out.

Dr. Emerson's hours were totally unpredictable, which made it hard for Eric to judge when to make his trip outside. That was only once a night and at that, not every night. Still, he did not want to run into Dr. Emerson, and none of this should effect the environment.

He hated the thought of still another report just now. All he wanted was to get the place thoroughly searched and get everyone out and buried. Then they could nose around all they wanted.

On the other hand, this was really his only duty. It was a cool job, and surely the alarms had nothing to do with his ancestors. He really had to tell Susan. Besides, she was the supervisor. She must know that the blips on the graphs meant a temperature deviation. If the temperature had not fluctuated, the whole system needed to be checked, just in case it was completely malfunctioning. Eventually, she would notice the blips and ask why he had failed to notify her. Then he would really be in hot water. He sighed and began to fill out a form.

Caleb Emerson had already written out his complaint report about the aberrant paging system. He had begun to write it several times before, but each time he was either interrupted or lost interest and did not turn it in.

Now, it was really driving him to distraction. He was coming in, because he was working on his project. Almost every night he was here, at least once, he got a page. The pages were usually wrong, but he could not ignore them. Sometimes they were real. Just the other night, he got one from a colleague in Siberia who was excavating a Scythian tomb.

This morning, at four a.m., there was a page to a Florida area code. Fearing his mother had been hospitalized, he returned the call. It was a donut shop in Cape Coral. That was the straw that broke the camel's back.

He noted a strong connection between the area, the time of day, and the malfunctions. "Whenever I come in early to get a good start on the day, I get these annoying pages. I can not discern the difference between a nonsense page and an emergency. I am fed up with talking to hospitals, pizza places, and operators. I insist this matter be cleared up immediately."

Someone had to fix this problem. That someone should be Susan. Thankfully, it was now her job to deal with idiots and idiosyncrasies.

Scattering another pile of papers, he found the complaint form. Then he headed directly to Susan's mailbox.

Susan took the forms in her stride initially. The alarm problem was getting old and she was still no closer to resolving it. In addition to Eric's reports, she had seen blips on the graphs and been talking to the alarm service for quite some time now. They had been out to check the system over three times already as a courtesy. She sensed that this was about the end of that charitable approach.

The other problem was the paging service. She had been expecting Dr. Emerson to send her a report about that problem, and here it was. The paging service was so efficient that she was sure there was nothing else they could possibly do. Still she had to call them as an official follow up.

"Hi, Joanne, it's Susan. Are you over that cold yet?"

"Pretty much, thanks for asking. How are you?"

"I'm okay, but I have this report from Dr. Emerson."

"Oh, dear," Joanne lamented. "I guess I should have been expecting that."

"Actually, he doesn't say anything we haven't discussed already, except that he insists we clear it up immediately. Those are his words not mine."

"He is the only complaint we have. We already issued him two brand new pagers and spare batteries," Joanne said hesitantly. "I can't think of what else to do."

Something in the tone of the last phrase alerted Susan. "Speaking off the record, do you have any idea what the problem is?"

"Don't you?"

"Not really, but I don't know much about the system. I would appreciate your suggestion, confidentially of course."

"Well," Joanne admitted. "Right from the beginning, I had my suspicions that it wasn't our system."

"Then what could it be?"

"You know him, what do you think?"

All Susan could think of was Dr. E. drinking the plant water. He was more than a little bizarre. "That it's all in his head?"

"That's an idea," Joanne conceded with a suspenseful drawl. "My conclusion - just between you and I - is that it's a prank."

"At that time of night?" Susan asked. "Who's awake at those hours?"

"Well," Joanne countered. "He's awake isn't he?"

"I guess so," Susan conceded. "But who and why?"

"As I said, you know him." Joanne said plainly. "If you were going to play a prank on someone, wouldn't he be the one?"

For the first time at that job, Susan laughed a good laugh.

"Face it," Joanne continued. "He's a pain in the you know where, and he's unpleasant to boot. When it comes to pranks, can you think of anyone more deserving?"

Stoically, Susan attempted to deal with each new problem as if it was a challenge. The approach was not working for her. That approach could not possibly work unless you were seriously delusional. Every problem in this place was utterly bizarre.

The computer however was working beautifully. Entering the data and dealing with the software was easy. Although that brought up another problem. The relics in the storehouse moved around. She knew they did; the shrunken heads and knives proved it. Besides that, the box packed with stuffed weasels was half empty, and there were two more boxes with stuffed weasels in them. She was pretty sure they were the same weasels. How many stuffed weasels could you have?

Boxes moved and the things inside of them moved. There were two incidents where boxes labeled pottery shards had switched contents. One had switched from pottery shards to bones. The other had switched from bones to fossilized rocks.

Once or two discrepancies, she could attribute to her own confusion, but there were too many times this had happened. Someone was moving things. The conclusion was inescapable. But who would want to do that? Why would they do this? It was not the kind of thing you did out of boredom. Everyone in the world, except for herself, had better things to do.

Doubtlessly, all of these artifacts had some value. At least, under the right circumstances, any relic could have some value. To the best of her knowledge, none of these had any value, and if they were not in a museum, they would be in a junkyard.

So what was this phantom searcher after? Could something here be valuable? Sometimes a new discovery threw a different light on an old one. It was a rarity, but it happened. It justified saving and preserving all of the artifacts here.

This presumption did not explain why things moved around or why there were more boxes and bins. Theft would result in fewer boxes, not more. Why were there more? Was someone hiding things? She had not run across anything that stood out or seemed to be contraband.

Who would move things, take things, or hide things in the storeroom? Only a limited number of people had access and none of them had a motive.

Dr. Joshua Moorland was in an unusually bad mood today. There was no particular reason; it was just a lousy day. It rained all morning, and he had a headache. The traffic was worse than usual, because there was another nuisance accident on the highway. His wife called to nag him.

Jeannie was in a good mood, which annoyed him even more. His desk held another whole set of problems. He had spent the morning on a tight schedule, full of meetings. There were new directives to look over. His voice mail was full; that had to wait a minute. There were some strange looking invoices on his desk.

The invoices were addressed to Susan. The services were complimentary for the most part. That was fine, but why did she have every possible repairman in existence coming to visit?

He had hired her to be less bother, not more. Now he had to

check on her. Just what he needed, another thing to do.

He punched in her extension number while he reviewed the rest of his mail. There was one reasonably official looking letter. It was another aggravation, the usual request from those local Indians. They wanted those skeletons back. There was no legal obligation here, but they kept on persisting.

Susan had the misfortune to answer her phone at that moment.

"Hello, Susan. How are you doing?"

"Hello, Dr. Moorland. I'm fine, thank you. How are you?"

"I'm just looking over some repair invoices," Dr. Moorland said testily. "I take it, you are you having problems..."

"Well, yes," Susan ventured. "Actually, the repairmen say everything is in good working order."

Joshua waited, but he did not get the information he wanted. "Then why the repair visits?" he snapped.

"Well, umm," Susan stammered hesitantly. "It looks a lot like we're having some alarm system malfunctions, but I guess we aren't." Now that she was started, the problems came flooding out. "I don't understand it, but they couldn't find anything wrong. The graphs were all off, and I was worried that the whole system was off. Then when they came to check, they said it was functioning fine. The paging system was causing Dr. Emerson some problems, so I had to have it checked out. They say everything is fine too. Really, right now, everything is just fine, I think."

He did not need this. "How's personnel?"

"Oh, they're all fine. I'll tell them you asked."

Idiot! Why had he hired her? "Have you started on the cataloging project?"

"Oh, ummm, yes," she replied uncertainly.

"Any problems with that?" he said sarcastically.

"Umm, well," Susan hedged. She was dying to tell him the problem, because she needed his help. But he was being so harsh, that she was reluctant. "Sort of, but I don't know if I should bother you with it just now. Maybe I should investigate more first."

"Yes, you should." At this point, he was exasperated. Surely, she could at least do the inventory right. "What is the problem?"

"The artifacts move."

"What do you mean?"

"When I inspect a container," Susan explained. "I note the label, contents, and location. A couple of days later, I reinspect that container, and something's changed."

Joshua knew this was ridiculous. "Can that be so?" he scoffed offhandedly.

"Yes, it can," Susan countered frankly. "Either someone's moving things around, or this storehouse is haunted."

"I see," Joshua replied shortly. He had no intention of dealing with this. He made a snap decision. "I have a new project for you. There has been a request from a local Native American organization. There are several skeletons of local Indians in the collection. They would like them returned for burial. This is a politically advantageous request for us to grant. I'll have a copy of it forwarded to you. The eight skeletons will have to be accounted for immediately, and all of the paperwork involved in the transfer needs to be completed by Wednesday."

"Wednesday?" Susan echoed with disbelief.

"Thank you, have a good evening." Joshua hung up the phone. This should solve the whole problem. Doubtlessly, she would fail, and he could justifiably fire her next week. Other problems needed his attention.

Ellen could not believe her good luck! She opened a book, and there was an article all about Eliza Loring Emerson!

The book was all about local history. In the back was a section profiling the more prominent people in the county. Apparently, she was very active in the community.

The article had all kinds of great information about her. Of course, it was in her husband's name. He was a very wealthy business man, but she sounded more interesting. Socially, she was active in conservative politics and charities. Their estate was a showplace, and they entertained frequently. Her writing was well received in literary circles. Most importantly, the article named all of their children.

Two sons were studying at prestigious colleges, and two daughters were well married. There was also mention of three younger children.

Her mission was to look up Eliza Loring and Henry West Emerson in the Census records. Since she had the names of the four older children, she could follow them through the Census records, too. This was an unbelievable piece of luck.

Susan felt totally overwhelmed by Dr. Moorland's request. How could she possibly account for eight relics by Wednesday? And he also wanted paperwork. What paperwork? She had not even found transfer forms yet. The whole matter gave her an insecure, sinking feeling.

It was the end of the day, and she could not collect her thoughts to figure out what to do. She looked around her office. It was starting to look so nice. Her desk was surrounded by Oriental screens. Her Tiffany desk lamp cast a warm glow. After a while, she went home to think.

Helpless, she felt helpless and confused. What could she do about this? Why did she have to have such an asshole for a boss? Why was he being so horrible to her?

At home, her first big decision was between wine and ice cream. Even that was too much for her to deal with right now.

She sat for a while and considered her job situation. What happened if she failed? She had a bad feeling she would be fired. Maybe it was all in her head, but what if that she was fired. Then again, was this really that great a job? What was she thinking? How long had she looked? Way too long, that was the answer. There were debts and bills... There was no choice. She had to make this job work.

Ice cream was her choice. Tonight she would fortify herself. Tomorrow she would begin the search. Even if it took all night, she would find those eight skeletons. As for the transfer forms, they had to be somewhere. Everything had to be somewhere.

The Emerson estate was simple but august. The buildings

were made of sprawling red brick. A tall black wrought iron fence and gate framed the entrance.

No member of the family could drive past the estate without stopping to look over their proud heritage. They particularly made a point of it when acquaintances were along. A touch of reflected fame and old money graces never hurt one's reputation.

This particular day the tour certainly had impact. Julia Emerson Franklin was out looking at property with her new husband and in-laws. They detoured to see the estate.

No one was home, but Julia, like all the relatives, felt free to walk around the grounds. Her new family was suitably impressed as she showed them the house, the gardens, and the carriage house. She always made a point of including the adjacent burying yard. It was absolutely not to be missed. Not only was it charmingly Yankee, but her most famous relations were buried there.

As they approached, Julia was looking the other way. She was busy finally making some points with her mother-in-law. Just as she was about to launch into her usual speech, she stopped, aghast at what she saw.

The burying ground was heaped with pile after pile of fresh dirt. It looked like a construction site. Almost a dozen graves were dug up! It was absolutely hideous!

The party stood, gaping dumbly, as their imaginations ran away with them. Even when they could speak, they did not want to say what they were thinking.

Julia thought she would faint. Which was worse, the trauma of seeing her relatives graves desecrated or the humiliation of it happening in front of her in-laws? She could not figure it out.

"I'm sure there's an explanation for this..." Was all Julia could offer her shocked guests. "My Auntie Meg will know."

Eric picked up the mail and his heart skipped a beat. There was a postmark from Sweden. He dropped everything else and grabbed it.

It was from Astrid. He scanned the letter with disbelief. Then he took a deep breath and sat down to read it in earnest.

'I know I owe to you an explanation, so here it is. I miss my home, and is as simple as that. America is nice, but it is not Sweden, and Sweden is home.

There's another thing I must tell you. I am pregnant with a daughter. I am not interested in marriage, but I am happy to be having a baby. She is your daughter, so I name her Ingar Ericson.

I am happy where I am. It's not a matter of I don't love you, but I can't ask you to leave your life for me. I would be happy to hear from you. I am sorry for any hurt, but you will get over me. Love Always, Astrid'

Eric was stunned. He sat thinking for what seemed like hours with his feelings churning inside.

Ingar Ericson! His daughter was going to be named Ingar Ericson! Traditionally, Scandinavian children are given their surname by adding 'son' to their fathers' first names. Eric's grandfather was named Lars, so his father's last name was Larson. His children would be named Ericson...

Astrid had released him from all obligation, but did she still love him? Did she want him to come to Sweden to be with her? Was this her way of saying good-bye? How could he tell?

'I can't ask you to leave your life for me.' Could he do that? Could he just drop everything and leave? Everything was here, his job, his family, his friends, and his place. How could he replace the life he had here?

The answer came quickly. Leaving would be easy. Suddenly, everything looked different. A few minutes ago he was content with his life here. Now it all seemed worthless. What life? He did not have a life keeping him here. What was he doing here besides smoking dope and guarding junk? There was not a reason in the world he should stay here.

He could get a pretty good job in Sweden. Certainly, his Uncle Sig would help him out with a fishing job. He could give his landlord a month's notice. Two weeks notice would be plenty for his job. When he thought about it, he had surprisingly few obligations to deal with here.

Only rescuing the ancestors needed to be finished up. There was time for that, unless he got caught.

If they noticed the skeletons missing later, being in Sweden would make life easier. They were not likely to chase him outside of the country. Besides, in Sweden, his name was Eric Johnson, because his father's name was John. They would never figure that out, and even if they did, there were thousands of Eric Johnsons.

Suddenly, he had a lot to do. There was packing, and sorting and reservations and storage and shipping. He needed to call his family. Should he call Astrid or surprise her? That was another decision.

Tonight he needed to find and rescue those last two ancestors. That meant he needed to call Melissa, too.

Chapter Seven

Rad paced testily. The acorns and squirrels were driving him crazy. Every ping and scratch reverberated on the tin roof. He knew it was just the tension of the situation getting to him. Despite the fact that he spent every day lounging, the anxiety was killing him. He was constantly listening for the police and watching the road. Fortunately, he did not have a television set there. It would have distracted him, and he would have been caught.

Now that he thought it over, he did not really have a good escape plan. What if the authorities did start down the road to his place? What would he do? It was a dead-end driveway. If they were coming in, he had no way out of there.

He would have to leave on foot or hide here. There were a couple of good crawl spaces they were unlikely to find. Unless they did a very thorough search, he would be safe. Eventually, they would find him if they were sure someone was hiding there, but he would have some time. The only problem was his truck. If they saw his truck there, they would know he was around.

There was another cabin not too far away if you went through the woods. The route there by road was roundabout. It was actually just as fast to walk. It was usually vacant, so he could hide the truck there. On the other hand, having it that far away, would keep him from making a quick getaway. Then again, he could hide there if he had to hide elsewhere. One way or another, he could make a plan out of this.

He decided to chance it and walk over to check it out. Putting on a loose shirt and green cap, he scanned to make sure no one was around. It seemed as good a time as any, so he started off into the woods.

It was wonderful to be outside in the woods. There nothing like sunlight and fresh air to cheer you up. He badly needed to relax. Maybe he should bag the idea of hiding and just go hiking and fishing. If he got caught, he got caught.

The path between the two cabins was overgrown, but he picked his way along without too much trouble. The trees were mostly pine and oak. Some of them were cathedral height. The sunlight broke through in brilliant shafts, illuminating the mossy rocks and underbrush. He strode slowly, taking in every detail and letting his spirit soar. When he stopped to look around, he realized this was a magical place.

Then the mosquitoes figured out he was there. He remembered now. They got really bad near that little swampy area in the middle. Usually, it did not bother him, because he was drunk. Now that he was sober, he found this truly unpleasant. These mosquitoes were nasty little creatures.

He hurried along to the neighbor's cabin. The guy who owned it was named Jeff. He was a good guy. They had gone fishing together a couple of times.

There was no vehicle there, but the driveway had new gravel on it. From the outside, it looked closed up. He found the spare key under its usual rock and went inside.

The first thing he did was open the refrigerator door. It was empty. There was no beer, therefore Jeff was not there. Steve sat down to think.

Very quickly, the decision became easy. There were even more acorns hitting Jeff's roof than his own.

Eric searched the storehouse with method and determination. Last night he had not had any luck at all. Tonight he had another area mapped out to search.

This was a total turn around from his initial random approach, but now time was of the essence. Astrid would not be pregnant forever. He needed to get there in a hurry. There were an amazing number of loose ends to tie up, and every minute needed to be put to good use.

Everything was different now that he had little Ingar Ericson to consider. As soon as he heard about her, he had stopped drinking and smoking dope without even trying. There was just no time for such foolishness anymore.

The minute the last person took their mop out the door, Eric started to comb the next room. About five minutes into his search, he noticed an odd thing. There were several totally unlabelled boxes right in a row. It struck him as peculiar. Most of the labels were wrong, but all of the other boxes, crates, and bins had at least some sort of label.

He opened the first box and was delighted to find a skeleton. Giving himself a pat on the back, he opened the second box and found another skeleton. Now he was suspicious. In all of his searching, he had not found two boxes containing exactly the same thing right next to each other except for pottery shards. There were so many of those it was inevitable some of them be next to each other, but there was only a sprinkling of skeletons.

He looked through the rest of the unlabeled boxes. All ten of them contained skeletons. There were only supposed to be eight Native American skeletons, and he had already found six of them. Something was wrong here.

He reexamined the boxes. Not only were the outsides unlabeled, there was no location of discovery or list of contents on the insides. There were no tags either. Usually, every individual artifact was tagged at least once just to keep its identity straight. The only identification he could find was a piece of paper with an illegible scrawl on it tossed in with the bones.

These skeletons were not part of the museum's collection. Eric was pretty clear on that. What were they doing here? Most importantly, were they Native American? How could you tell?

Dr. Emerson's office would have a book on that matter. Fortunately, he had a pass key. He let himself in and looked around. Dr. Emerson had a lot of interesting books. He snagged a likely one and went back to the shelf.

He examined each skull carefully. All of them were Caucasian except for one. That one was questionable. It was not as definitely Caucasian as the others. It looked somewhat Native American, but not an archetype. Of course, he was not an expert, but what to do? Should he take it or leave it?

Eric put a little blue pen mark on that box and put it at the edge of the group. Since it was with the other Caucasian skeletons, he felt it was not one of the ones he was trying to find. On the other hand, ancestors were ancestors, weren't they?

What were all of these skeletons doing here? Unless a local cemetery had been moved. They could have been stored here temporarily and forgotten. It was absurd, but that must be it. Why else would they be here? Didn't the people from this community care about their ancestors? Should he care about them?

He had to think over that one questionable skeleton. If they had been a part of the White society, did he care? He wasn't sure. He would consult Melissa and think on it.

Susan got an early start on the day. She was going to find those skeletons. Whatever it took, she had to find them. There was no choice in the deal.

Systematically, she began probing every box on every shelf, nook and cranny of the place. As she searched, she marked it off. Until she was done there would be no stopping.

Her resolution lasted until lunch. She just had to put her feet up. Worst of all, she had hardly made a dent in the place. For her break, she had a sandwich and a very large coffee. Then it was back to the grind.

Several hours later, she gave up for the night. She was exhausted, filthy, and her arms ached. This was not an efficient use of her energy. Dinner, bed, and bath were in order.

Eric and Melissa finished the last meditation of the burial service. Together they got up and began to sing as they rhythmically shoveled soil into the new grave. Mostly Melissa sang. The words were beginning to make sense to her. Eric tried to keep up and chime in as best he could.

When they finished, Eric nodded to Melissa. "Every service gets better, Sis."

"Thanks," she said happily. That holy feeling was back, and it was very strong.

"You're getting good with the words and all," Eric observed.

"An interesting thing is happening," Melissa began. Then a feeling swept over her, and she stopped. "You've heard from

Astrid," she stated firmly.

"Yeah," Eric said with surprise. "How'd you know?"

"I'm not sure how," Melissa said. "Suddenly I just knew. That's the kind of interesting thing that keeps happening."

"You know things?"

"Yes," Melissa said plainly. "I think something, and it happens. Before I pick up the phone, I know who it is. It's strange, but I like it."

"You're turning psychic?" Eric asked. "Do you think it has to do with Aunt Mae's lessons?"

"I guess so," Melissa answered. "It started at the same time I began the meditations she taught me. I'll tell you more when I understand it better. What's happened with Astrid?"

"I got a letter from her." Eric took a deep breath. "I'm going to be a father!"

Melissa was speechless. So much for knowing things before they happened.

"She doesn't say any of the important things," Eric told her somberly, "like when she's due or if she knew she was pregnant when she left. She's staying in Sweden, that's for sure."

"What are you going to do?" Melissa asked. No matter how she tried, she simply could not picture her little brother being a father.

"I've thought things through as best I can." Eric did not know how to tell Melissa his decision. "It took a lot of soul searching, but I've decided. I'm moving to Sweden as soon as possible."

"But, Eric," Melissa protested. "You said you hated it there. Don't you recall saying something like you'd never go back unless your plane crashed there?"

"Well, yes, that's true," Eric admitted. "That was right after Greta broke my heart. The place doesn't matter. The point is, I need to be with Astrid."

"So, she asked you to come and join her?" Melissa prompted eagerly. Why did it take him so long to tell the story?

"Nooo, not exactly," Eric said thoughtfully. "The way I look at it, she didn't have to tell me where she was or that she was pregnant. I think she wants me to prove that I want to be with her."

"Do you?" Melissa asked.

"Yes, I do," Eric said firmly. "At first, I wasn't sure. I didn't know what to think. When I thought it over, it was obvious. My new family to be is in Sweden. Of course I should be with them."

"Congratulations," Melissa said tentatively. What else could she possible say to him? She had never been able to see Eric and Astrid together, but nothing ever seemed to break them up. He was doing the honorable thing and stranger couples had lasted together.

"I know what you're thinking," Eric said.

"I didn't say anything..."

"You didn't have to," Eric countered. "Astrid and I do fight a lot. I know we have stuff to iron out, but we've been doing it. I have something with her, that I don't have with anyone else. She's worth the compromises, really she is."

"You don't have to talk to me about compromises." Melissa almost giggled. She remembered talking about Rad this way. Where did time go?

"I knew that you of all people would understand." Eric started to laugh, too. "I figure it this way. She's the one who has to have the baby. She ought to be able to have it anywhere she wants to."

"Are you happy about it?" Melissa pried.

"I guess so," Eric said. "You know, they've always said I was an underachiever who lacked motivation. Having a family is suddenly a pretty big motivation. I feel that I've been wasting my life away, and it's about time I did something."

Melissa stared at him intensely. "Are you feverish? I've never heard you talk this way before."

"Things are different now," Eric explained proudly. "I have a family to support. Do you think I should ask Astrid to marry me as soon as I arrive or should I buy her a ring first?"

"If you really want to impress her," Melissa said mischievously. "You'll have the ring when you arrive."

Eric looked at her. With all his expenses, how was he going to do that?

"You know I'm right," Melissa admonished. "But, if you have to pick, propose immediately."

"Yeah," Eric said. "You're right. I considered calling her, but I'm just going to show up and hopefully sweep her off her feet. I'm leaving as soon as I finish things up here."

"What do you need to finish up?"

"Just burying the ancestors and packing my stuff, which brings me to another point."

"Let me guess," Melissa sighed. "You want me to dig two holes next week."

"Yeah, that's right," Eric confirmed, "presuming I find them. Also there's been another development. I found a stray skeleton that might be one of ours. I don't know what to do."

"A stray skeleton? What's that?"

"Everything in the museum's collection is boxed and tagged and labeled," Eric explained. "This skeleton isn't tagged at all. Not only that, I can't tell if it's Caucasian or Native American. It's in a line of untagged Caucasian skeletons. I think they might be from an old graveyard that they forgot about. So I'm not sure if we should bury it or not."

"So, now you want me to dig three holes?" Melissa asked suspiciously. "Is that what you're getting at?"

"Maybe... I'm not sure." Eric hesitated. How could he explain it? "It's easy to figure out what to do with the Native American skeletons that were found in excavations, because I'm sure all of them would like to follow tradition and be buried in the earth. My first reaction is to bury this other person too, but I'm not sure she followed her native traditions."

"I see what you mean," Melissa said thoughtfully. "Those other skeletons she's next to might be her family and her friends. Maybe she'd rather stay with them. I think you should leave that one."

Eric thought it over. "I think you're right. What's for breakfast?"

Caleb arrived home and had dinner before he checked his messages. His mother had left an unusually pleasant request for him to call her. He settled down with a glass of Cognac and called her.

"Hello dear," his mother answered cordially. "How are you?"

"Fine, Mother," Caleb said absently, "just fine. What's the occasion for the call?"

"I just wondered what had been going on."

"Oh, nothing to speak of. How about you?"

"Are you sure?" Her voice became penetrating.

"Uh, yes," Caleb stumbled. "Why?"

"Because Caleb," she snapped. "The jig is up! I got a call from your cousin, Julia."

He could not imagine what she was getting at. "And what did she have to say?"

"You don't know do you?" Meg Emerson was totally exasperated with her son.

"No, I don't," Caleb answered firmly. "Stop playing games, Mother."

"Your cousin stopped by last week to show off the house to her new in-laws," she explained pointedly. "Certainly you can imagine how mortified she was to find out that she was related to a grave robber."

"That's not really so..." Caleb began to deny.

"She said the entire burying ground was dug up!" Meg almost screamed. "What do you have to say for yourself?"

Caleb's stomach sank, and he thought fast. "Mother, I'm landscaping."

"What!" Meg gasped. That was the most ridiculous lie she had ever heard in her life!

"I'm landscaping," he explained. "That's why it's a mess."

"You are not landscaping," Meg contradicted bluntly. "You wouldn't know a hemlock from a forsythia."

"Yes, I would," Caleb insisted. "Forsythia are deciduous."

"Deciduous!" Meg repeated furiously. "The harbinger of spring and you describe it as deciduous?"

"Well, it is," Caleb said mildly.

"Caleb, it is no use denying it," Meg said squarely. "You are my son and I love you, but you are a very weird man. You have never been interested in anything alive, only in things that are dead. If you'll recall, you lost three wives over it."

"That's not so," Caleb contradicted. "They just didn't understand the hardships of being married to an archaeologist."

"Yes, they did," Meg insisted sternly. "They expected the burning sands of Egypt and the malaria ridden jungles of Brazil. Each of them was willing to sacrifice, all for the sake of knowledge and treasure. What they didn't expect was being repeatedly forgotten at airports, hotels, and laundromats. Three brilliant, cultured women have left you because you totally ignored them for your work."

"Mother, please...." Caleb groaned. He did not want to hear about this subject again.

"Caleb," Meg continued relentlessly, "if there are holes in the burying ground, it is doubtlessly because you have been digging up bodies. I am your mother, and I know you, so don't argue with me. "

"If you would let me explain..."

"No, I don't want to hear it." His mother cut him off sharply. "Don't say anything else, you'll only make it worse. I am shocked and appalled and repulsed, because I have a reasonable idea of what you were thinking. How you could experiment on your relatives is utterly beyond me. I am catching a flight home on Friday evening. On Sunday, I will supervise the reburial of the family."

"Just wait a minute here, Mother," Caleb sputtered. "I am a grown man, and you can't treat me this way."

"You'll do what I say, or I'll disinherit you."

"Nonsense," Caleb protested firmly. "The family won't stand for it."

"They will," Meg threatened darkly, "as soon as they realize they'll get to divide up your share. You know I'm right about this."

"Yes, Mother," Caleb conceded. "You are right about that. I'll pick you up on Friday."

"You'd better." Meg hung up the telephone deliberately.

Caleb was infuriated. How could she interrupt his study this way? The whole conversation grated. How dare she threaten him! He had not even had a chance to tell her about the tests he was running and the historical picture that was forming. That was the part he resented most. Of all the rotten luck, why had some of the family come by just now? Another month and they would never even have noticed. He just could not bring the study to a halt. There were still a few days left, and he was determined to finish up.

Susan made it through the first half of Monday searching frantically. All weekend, she had searched diligently. Since then she had not eaten or slept properly. She was exhausted and her nerves were bad. It was all on the line, and the pressure was breaking her.

When she checked her voice mail, there was a testy message from Dr. Moorland. She went right over the edge and started to cry with fatigue and frustration. The injustice was too much!

Who were these people to take this hard earned job from her? It was Dr. Moorland she wanted to yell at, but she could not possibly yell at Dr. Moorland. She would definitely be fired for that.

What about these Indians? After all these years, to suddenly make this ridiculous demand... She checked the letter to see who she should curse. Their office was right down the street.

A crazy thought surfaced. Maybe if she went to their office and talked to the Indians face to face she could reason with them to give her more time. That would lift the pressure from Moorland and in turn give her a break. It was a totally inappropriate idea, but she was desperate. How could it hurt?

Caleb was dismayed at the new development. Now he had to hurry to complete his tests. Today he could get the last of them sent off. He reviewed his list and got busy.

The next problem was getting the bones back out of the storehouse. It should not be a big deal, but he could not very well walk out the door with ten crates. Or could he? If he put them in file boxes, he could say that they were his personal files. Yes, he would mention it to Joshua. Then he could probably get that security guard to help him.

Susan barged into Joe's office. "I'm Susan Slater from the museum," she announced.

He looked up from his cup of herbal tea, and it was obvious she had disturbed him. Suddenly, she realized how she looked and became self-conscious. She was haggard and disheveled. There were probably dirt streaks on her face.

"Please have a seat," Joe motioned to her. What could he do for her? She had a wild-eyed look about her. Then again, she may have just received a box of one of her relatives' bones. He had better handle her with kid gloves.

"I know you weren't expecting me, but I'm here," she stammered.

"What can I do for you? Maybe a cup of tea?" Joe asked.

"I'm working as hard as I can," Susan said angrily. "I just want you to know that. You just haven't given me enough notice. The whole place is a mess. It's total turmoil - half the labels are wrong. Worse yet I think it's haunted, because things keep moving around."

"Is that so?" Joe began to think she was simply a nut case. What was she talking about?

"If I can't find your skeletons," Susan ranted, "it's because they don't want to be found. Maybe when they're gone I'll be able to sort out everything."

Joe tried to placate her. "Susan, do you realize..."

"I just have to ask for more time," Susan interrupted frantically. "It's waited all these years, surely another week won't matter."

"Susan, I don't know..." Joe tried to explain again.

"I really need this job. It took me so long to find it. Moorland will fire me, and I can't get fired. I'll never get another job. I'll keep looking and return all eight skeletons just as soon as I find them."

Eight skeletons made it dawn on Joe what she was talking about. Now he understood why the museum did not return the

Wampanoag skeletons. They could not find them. "All right, another week is fine with me."

"All right?"

"Yes, it's all right," Joe said calmly. "You don't need to have a nervous breakdown. We appreciate your hard work."

"What a relief. Dr. Moorland insisted on Wednesday."

"We haven't spoken," Joe said curiously.

"Then you didn't insist on Wednesday?" Susan asked.

"No, if Dr. Moorland calls me, I'll tell him the end of the month will be fine."

"Then, I have to get back to work," Susan said. She was starting to feel stupid. "We'll be in touch, okay?"

"Okay."

Eric kept searching the storehouse methodically. He had one large room left to go through. Instead of meandering like he used to in the beginning, he hurried along.

Then he found them! They were not right together, but they were close. Quickly, just in case there were any more skeletons, he combed the rest of the room. The night was almost over when he took the two skeletons out to the truck.

Eric was ecstatic when he left work. His mission was complete. All of his ancestors had been rescued. All he really needed to work out now was when to give his notice. Time versus money was the question. He would need as many paychecks as he could get for the new start.

Melissa was already meditating when he arrived. He did not want to break her concentration, so he unloaded the skeletons quietly beside her.

"I'm going to miss these ceremonies," Melissa said solemnly. "I've made a decision."

"What's that?"

"I'm going to become a traditional healer," Melissa announced proudly.

"That's great," Eric said. "What about Rad?"

"I'm sure he'll approve," Melissa replied.

"I meant, have you heard from him?"

"Oh, no, I haven't," Melissa said. "I'm sure he's okay. I just know it. It sounds strange, but at night, I can feel him lying in bed thinking of me."

"You're getting pretty serious about this stuff," Eric observed dubiously.

"This is very exciting!" Melissa protested. "Aunt Mae is going to introduce me to a healer. If all goes well, I'm going to study with her."

"That is exciting," Eric agreed. He had never seen Melissa act like this. Usually with Rad gone this long, she would be falling apart with worry. Instead, she had a calm air about her. "I'm going to miss you, Sis."

"Oh, Eric!" Melissa jumped up and hugged him. "You better come back and visit a lot."

Susan found the situation confusing, so she tried to think it through. It was clear that for whatever reason, Moorland was unhappy with her. That was why he set this deadline. He wanted her to fail so that he would have an excuse to get rid of her.

She was so mad that she felt like crying. What had she done to deserve this? She was doing what he had assigned her. He was no support whatsoever. What did he want?

What was her future? If she was able to stay around, it was pretty grim. She had to get past this and look for another position.

In the meantime, it was back to poking through boxes. She was so tired she was getting punchy. Being depressed and exasperated did not help.

Then it happened. She found a skeleton! There was no proper identification, but she examined the bones. From what she knew about it, the skeleton looked Native American. She pulled out her college notes. It looked more or less Native American. This had to be one of them!

The next box contained another skeleton. It was like a gold mine. Box after box contained skeletons. She counted them down until she got to eight. At eight, she jumped for joy.

That was it! They had all been together! That was why she could not find any of them before. But now she had them all. Immediately, she locked them in her office.

It was very late, but it was still Tuesday. In the morning, she could design an 'updated' transfer form for Dr. Moorland. Tonight she was celebrating with a bubble bath, a microwave dinner, and a good night's sleep.

Ellen was ready to celebrate. She fixed some hors d'oeuvres and opened a bottle of Champagne. It was a tradition with her. Whenever she cracked a tough case, she started the celebration with Champagne, then she enjoyed a gourmet meal with a friend. Tonight it would be a female friend, more was the pity, but you never knew who you would meet out on the town.

She had successfully tracked the Loring-Emerson family up to the present. The Emersons were prominent enough that it was easy to follow their line. They almost always had little blurbs written about them in directories. Their obituaries were always very informative.

Best of all, this might be the right family. There were two mentions of Indian relics in different wills. It was always a triumph to complete a family tree.

In a way, she hoped that this was the family with the relics. Her client would be happy and might hire her again if another project came up. She could at least count on an excellent reference.

On the other hand, the longer she searched, the more money she made from this case. No one would be likely to acknowledge the receipt of a stolen item like the Wampum Belts, so maybe she would get both wishes.

Chapter Eight

Steve felt like he was really starting to enjoy himself and adjust to life at the cabin. The stress and tranquillity were balancing out. He was getting used to keeping a watchful eye on the road while tuning out the acorns.

He spent the evening reading in front of the fire. Usually, he read books about his people and their struggles. Lately, he was tired of reading about Native Americans struggling with White invaders. What he really wanted to read about were Native Americans without conflict from other races. It was always in there, at least as a backdrop. There were a thousand universal stories that could be told, but they were all ignored in lieu of that one.

He also liked classics for a change of pace, so tonight's pick was 'Oliver Twist'. He was going to bypass it, because the movies made it a children's book. Nothing could be further from the truth. It centered on lowest class criminals and their personal ethics. Steve thought it was insightful.

That night, he fell into a good sleep, despite the acorns. The sound of a hound dog baying roused him. Then barking, snarling and a trash can turning over jolted him awake.

Steve jumped up and looked out the window. The neighbor's dog had cornered a raccoon on top of the garbage cans. He decided not to interfere. Let them settle their own problems.

Some time later, he was awakened by a presence. It was the raccoon. He could hear it scuffling around the cabin while the dog bayed and snuffled outside. Apparently, the desperate raccoon got in a window with a ripped screen. Maybe the raccoon ripped a screen. It was hard to say.

As much as Steve liked wildlife, he was not crazy about sharing his sleeping quarters with them. Once he realized the animal was inside, he was wide awake. His first instinct was to shoo it back out, but he knew better than to try. The raccoon was frantic. he waited for it to settle down and inadvertently fell back to sleep.

The raccoon found the pantry and naturally ripped up the bag of flour and a box of saltine crackers. Then it knocked over several cans and broke a jar of beets. That woke Steve back up with a start again. He decided to take a stab at animal psychology. Calmly he opened the front door and stepped away to let the raccoon outside. The dog promptly came barreling in and ran right for the pantry.

The raccoon holed up in a cabinet. The huge dog tried barging in the door. Steve grabbed a broom and swatted the dog until he ran back outside. He closed the front door and the cabinet door and went back to bed.

Caleb felt grouchy this morning. Last night was a restless, miserable night. Here he was a grown man with his mother bossing him around like a child. He seethed whenever he thought about capitulating. She still held the purse strings, and he had to respect that. Living on his salary as a professor was a bleak thought.

Additionally, he was aware that by and large, most people would find his study shocking and condemn him heartily. So, he dug up his own relatives to study them. So what? They were interesting.

It was truly a double standard, and worse yet, it was an utterly ridiculous one. After all, it was his business to excavate ancient civilizations in order to study them. That included graves. Most people were so very impressed that he was an archaeologist. The study of mankind and bygone civilizations fascinated them. Why did it horrify them to study their own bygone civilizations?

It was such petty emotional nonsense. He reminded himself that every ancient civilization had had its own set of ludicrous superstitions. Why should contemporary civilizations be any different?

Caleb sighed to himself. Philosophy had to be put aside for a later time. He needed to pave the way for reburial of his specimens.

When he had a few quiet minutes, Caleb fabricated an excuse to speak with Joshua. Whether or not they should both attend a luncheon was the initial topic.

It was easy enough to get off on a more personal topic. He chose an invitation to the family clambake near the end of the summer. Traditionally, it was held at his place, since it was an estate. Friends of the family were always on the invitation list. A note would have sufficed, but the invitation was sincere.

"Naturally," Caleb said. "I've been doing some work on the place to get ready for the festivities. Joshua, you and Bess just have to put this on your calendar. I think you're always delightful company to mix in with the Emersons."

"I'll have to talk to Bess before I commit us," Joshua replied, "but it sounds good to me."

"You'll be getting a formal invitation," Caleb said smoothly. "I just haven't gotten to it. I've been busy cleaning out all of my files here and at home. Some of them, I need to move into proper storage. What's that new administrator's name?"

"Susan Slater?"

"Yes, that's the one. I need her to get one of the guards to give me a hand moving the dead files out one night this week."

"If she's still around by the end of the week," Joshua said bluntly. "I'm sure that'll be fine."

"She's leaving?"

"Let's say she's not working out as anticipated," Joshua informed him. "She just can't handle things. For example, she's had the alarm people out here to check the system, and nothing's wrong with it. Then she claims someone is moving the relics in the storage areas around. Ridiculous!"

"That's too bad," Caleb said quickly to cover his pang of conscience. "She seemed promising enough."

"I have to be going. I'll get back to you about the clambake."

"Very good."

Caleb hung up. He hoped he was not responsible for her confusion about relics in the storage areas. On the other hand, the alarms had never caused him any trouble. She would have to sink or swim on her own. He had his own problems.

He dialed Susan's phone number. "This is Dr. Emerson," he

told her voice mail. "Could I have one of the security people give me a hand moving out some files this week? Thank you."

The people part of it was covered. Now he needed to move the boxes into his office, repack them and sort some real files. He turned the corner to where he had stored the skeletons and stared. The shelf was empty. Only two of the ten skeletons were there.

For a moment, his mind went blank. Panic stricken, he put the last two skeletons in his office. He sat to try and sort it out, but his head spun. what could have happened? Who would take eight skeletons? He tried to think clearly. The only person that he could think of that might be moving things around was Susan. He needed to get to the bottom of this right now.

As he headed towards Susan's office, he saw her in the hall.

"Oh, Susan," he hailed.

Susan was surprised to hear him speak to her. After the first week, she had given up on saying hello to him.

"Dr. Emerson," she acknowledged pleasantly.

"There's a matter I need to ask you about," he said working hard at staying calm.

"If it's about the guard helping you," Susan replied efficiently. "It's all squared away."

"Thank you," Caleb said impatiently. "But I wanted to know about something else. There's a storage room near my office with an entire shelf suddenly vacant. What's going on?"

"That's where the skeletons were for those Indians," Susan said. It struck her as peculiar that Dr. Emerson noticed, but then he was peculiar. "Dr. Moorland's having us return them to the local Wampanoag tribe."

"What?" Dr. Emerson asked. The idea of returning relics to the locals was preposterous.

"Dr. Moorland said it had to be done by today, and it is!" Susan declared triumphantly. "I've got all of the eight skeletons locked up in my office, and the paperwork is right here." She waved it happily.

"That can't be!" Dr. Emerson stated harshly. This was unbelievable! She had his skeletons! Worse yet, they were being given away. He would either have to resign or be disinherited.

"To whom are they going?"

"To the organization on this request right here," Susan waved it happily. She didn't know what Dr. Emerson's problem was, but her job was safe. "Dr. Moorland said that politically, it was very important that the museum return them immediately."

"Could I have a copy of that?" Dr. Emerson asked angrily. "Here I'll scribble it down."

Caleb made a frantic exit. This situation was outrageous! What to do now? Joshua knew perfectly well that he did not have any local projects at the moment or even in the near future. What possible reason could he have for even displaying interest in the subject?

He looked at the name of the organization. The Wampanoags were local. Last he heard, they were not nationally recognized. There was no legal obligation to return any skeletons. The very thought of giving away anything rubbed him the wrong way. That was simply not how museums worked.

If Joshua said it was politically advantageous, then it must be important. What could he do? If he identified them as Caucasian, he made the museum look stupid. If he told Joshua the truth, he would be asked to resign, albeit quietly, for unauthorized exhumation. If he did nothing...

This was very bad. The only party left were the Indians. He had to negotiate with them and buy his boxes of bones back.

Ellen settled down with a cup of tea at the computer. She loved the computer. It organized things so beautifully. Right now, she needed to summarize the Loring file.

First she entered the family tree. The program gave her a clear graphic representation of every generation. That was her favorite part.

Then she needed to compose the text. This was the boring part. Every statement had to have a reference to a document of some kind. She had a pretty standard format for that, but this case was different. Usually, she traced backwards from the client. The Wampanoag cases started well in the past, and she traced them to the present. It took a little doing, but her usual format worked pretty well backwards.

She was so excited, she just could not wait to see Joe. Two wills had mention of Indian beadwork. This had to be the family. What else would you pass down in a will?

Joe sat at his desk nursing a cup of tea and wishing it was coffee. He was tired. Yesterday's visitor disturbed him, and he had not slept well. His dreams were full of frazzled people and dark labyrinths.

This was another day, and there were decisions to make. Cheerful sunlight beamed through the window, and he began to make some progress. Then the interruption barreled in.

"I'm Dr. Caleb Russell Emerson, and I need to speak to you about the skeletons."

Joe sized him up. This man was upset and angry. He was not outwardly angry, but it was very likely that he was the recipient of Rad's political statement.

"Have a seat." Joe gestured cautiously.

Caleb smoldered, but he sat.

"I'm Joe Green." Joe tried to be as cordial as possible. "What can I help you with?"

"It's about the skeletons," Dr. Emerson said tensely.

Joe was not sure whether he meant Rad's skeletons or Susan's skeletons, so he did not reply.

"The skeletons," Dr. Emerson said haltingly, "are not yours." He hated spelling this out.

"What do you mean?" Joe still wanted the whole explanation. It was the best way to buy time in a public relations crisis.

"I mean," Caleb said through gritted teeth, "that the skeletons they are going to give you, aren't from Indians, uh, Native Americans. You simply can't accept them."

Now that it was clear they were discussing the museum's skeletons, Joe considered the matter with relief.

"How do you know that?" Joe asked pointedly. Susan seemed a little unstable, but she also seemed honest.

"Because I am an archaeologist," Caleb almost yelled. Why

were they questioning him? Then he remembered what was at stake and recovered, "And I am affiliated with the museum."

Obviously something was at stake besides the museum's reputation or the rest of Wampanoag souls. Joe needed more information.

"Why would they try to deceive us?" Joe asked.

"No, we would never do that," Dr. Emerson sputtered. "This is just a tragic mistake. The incompetent woman in charge, Susan, has set aside the wrong skeletons to give back to you. They aren't yours. They're mine, and I need them to complete a project."

Joe looked at Dr. Emerson steadily, waiting to hear what was really going on. If this were a legitimate matter, a bigwig like Dr. Emerson would have gone through official channels at the museum.

"I have to get them back right away." Caleb began to feel desperate. He was not making any progress here. "I should never have dug them up. Surely there's some kind of deal we can make or agreement we can come to."

"I don't see how I can help you," Joe told him calmly. "Whenever possible we try to regain the bones of our ancestors..."

"They're not your ancestors." Caleb began to rant. "That's what I'm trying to tell you. This has nothing to do with your ancestors. These are my ancestors, and I'll be disinherited if I don't get them back!"

"You dug up your own ancestors?" Joe stared in shock. How could anyone do such a terrible thing?

"I'm an archaeologist!" Caleb explained defensively. "I dig up everybody's ancestors."

Joe was silent trying to accept this. Would a person really dig up their own family? Apparently he had, but this was unbelievably macabre.

"Don't you see," Dr. Emerson demanded. "I'm in terrible trouble here. I need the eight skeletons that are on their way to you."

"Because they are your ancestors' skeletons?" Joe said to stop him. What was he going to dream tonight after dealing with this ghoul?

"Exactly!" Caleb felt Joe finally understood the situation. "And, I have to rebury them where they belong."

"You dug up your own relatives?" Joe repeated. He just could not get past this.

"Yes, I already said that," Caleb said impatiently. "I am doing a study."

"So what do you want me to do?" Joe asked hesitantly.

"Make a deal," Caleb said bluntly. "Surely I could buy them from you. There must be a reasonable price for something you don't even want."

Joe had no idea what to think of this. He was still stuck on the idea of digging up relatives. He needed to think this over, but there was no time, and Caleb talked continually.

"First of all," Joe said slowly. "I don't have anything to trade you for yet. Secondly, I will have to think the matter over before I consider striking a deal. Where can I reach you?"

Caleb suddenly felt spent. "I have a business card."

Melissa sang as she raked the soil and scattered the seeds. Then she smoothed it over and sang another prayer over it. At first she felt a little silly, but Aunt Mae told her to follow the healer's directions to the word.

The healer hardly said anything to her. She gave Melissa a packet of seeds to plant. Some of the seeds she recognized and some she didn't. Melissa presumed they were medicinal plants, and that she needed to learn how to grow them. It was a slow first step, but she suspected the whole project was going to be a slow one.

Melissa finished the prayers and continued into the meditations. Meditation was coming much more easily to her. As she spent more time meditating, her outlook changed. She was much calmer and happier than she ever was before.

She became more trusting of her intuition. Her intuition was getting stronger and stronger. Inanimate objects started to have personalities. Places had feelings. She could feel a person's soul. It was very strange, but she tried to honor it.

As she passed through the woods, it seemed to be its own being. She passed slowly by the eight grave sites. Each one had its own individual spirit. Every time she passed it, she felt they all were thanking her.

She wished Rad were there to experience this with her. Usually, she would be falling apart being separated from him for this long. Now she missed him, but she was managing just fine without him.

An idea crossed her mind and she decided to go with it. She sat down right on the spot and meditated. Then she thought about Steve or rather she thought to Steve. She felt that she could see him and feel his presence. He was safe, but he was also unhappy and bored and irritable. Just for an instant, she joined him and pictured herself telling him to come home.

When that meditation was over, she felt tired and drained. She decided to have a cup of herbal tea and do something analytical.

Eric came in very early to give his notice. Two weeks was adequate monetarily. Uncle Sig called last night with a job offer for the fall, so the sooner, the better.

Usually, he would have told Dr. Emerson, but Dr. Emerson was only around when you did not want him. Susan was his next choice.

He rapped on her door and entered. "Hi, Susan, remember me? I'm Eric Larson."

"Yes, come on in."

"Actually," Eric said politely. "I'm here to give my notice. I'm moving in two weeks."

"I'm sorry to hear that," Susan said professionally. "How long have you been here?"

"About a year," Eric surveyed her cluttered office. "What are all of those boxes?"

"Dr. Moorland had a project for me," Susan explained proudly. "I had to find all of these skeletons so they can be given to some local Indian group."

Eric thought his jaw was going to hit the ground. All he

could do was stand there stupidly.

"All day and all night," Susan complained happily. "I've been looking for old Indian skeletons. After all of these years, you'd think no one would care anymore. According to the files, the most recent one was donated before 1910, and they all died over two hundred years before that."

Eric was still stunned. This was all wrong.

"But, the great Dr. Moorland," Susan said sarcastically, "has said that they must go back, and so they must." She realized that this was an attitude not befitting a manager, but Eric was leaving in two weeks. "Supposedly, there's some political advantage to returning them. Quite frankly, I'm sure they were only donated by alumni for a tax deduction, and only accepted as a favor to them. I can't imagine what use they are to anyone."

"So, uh, have you found... How many have you found... so far?"

"I have all eight," Susan said beaming. "This week, I killed myself looking for them. It's so hard to find a decent job these days, I had to push myself to the limit. I actually thought Dr. Moorland was going to fire me over this. When I was desperate, I suddenly found all eight at once."

Eric made his excuses and went back to his post. He did not know what to think. It was weird enough to think the museum would actually return these skeletons after all this time. Now, Susan says she has all eight skeletons. She couldn't possibly have them, because he had already buried them. He had checked every box in every room. He had absolutely all the Native American skeletons.

Then he remembered that there were several Caucasian skeletons in that one section. He checked that room. The boxes of Caucasian skeletons were gone, so those must be the ones in Susan's office. What, if anything at all, should he do now?

He spent a lot of the night thinking about it. It disturbed him to feel this dishonest. He had not intended for anyone to get into trouble over this. If he came forward and said what he had done, he would probably end up in jail. He just could not let that happen, not with a new daughter to think about.

If he pointed out that the skeletons were Caucasians once

114

they were returned, Susan would be in trouble. He felt that was unfair, besides eventually someone would ask where the eight Native American skeletons were.

The museum would have egg on its face when they could not find the Native American skeletons, but he was ambivalent about that. Sure, they gave him a cool job, but that was a job. It was a fair deal, work for pay. What would have happened to the skeletons if the museum had not accepted them? Would they have been reburied or used as Halloween decorations? Who knew?

The point was that the museum should not have kept them. They should have returned them to the Wampanoag descendants as soon as they were asked. If the museum was embarrassed by this, they were only getting their just deserves.

So far the best option was to do nothing at all, but the ramifications of that bothered him, too. His own people would bury the wrong skeletons. These Caucasians, who in life had probably hated all Indians and stolen their land, would be getting an honorable burial by Wampanoags. He could not stand that idea either.

The real Wampanoag ancestors that he had rescued were safely buried, but no one would ever know that. It was only his own people that mattered. As he thought it through, he had to do something. There had to be someone he could tell.

Steve rolled over and groaned. It was daylight, and still more acorns were showering the roof. Why did they seem louder when he was tired?

It was nice outside, and it was well into the day. The squirrels were awake and driving him crazy. Every time one of them landed on the roof, he jumped. It sounded like they weighed about twenty pounds.

He might as well get up. Steve opened the kitchen and pantry windows. Then he let the raccoon out of the cabinet and stood back until it scurried out the window.

What a mess! Pink flour and crumbs were plastered all over the kitchen. The floor was totally covered with it. There were paw prints all over the table, the windows, and the curtains. Scrubbing down the kitchen was the last thing he had planned for today.

He started the coffee and looked down the road hopefully. There was no sign of the authorities. If the FBI was going to come and get him, this would be a good time.

He was tired and bored. Nature was driving him crazy. There was a whole list of things he missed. Hot water and Melissa topped the list although not necessarily in that order.

As he thought of Melissa for just a second, he thought she was standing next to him. Her presence was so strong, he could smell her scent. It startled him, and then she was gone. He must miss her more than he realized.

Suddenly, he decided to give it up. He needed to see Melissa. Police or not, he was going home right away. Realistically, he was going just as soon as he had coffee and cleaned up the flour and beet juice.

Joe gave in, and resorted to coffee today. He needed to shake the disturbing presence of that archaeologist. Again, his sleep had been disrupted, and he was tired. He had work to do, and he needed to concentrate. Hopefully, the coffee would help.

How could you dig up your own relatives? The image of it appeared in his dreams last night, and it still haunted him in the daylight. His reaction alternated between disgust and horror.

Why would you dig them up? To study them? What could you possibly study that was that interesting?

The archaeologist wanted to trade or buy the bones back. Joe wondered about that and concluded it must be blackmail. Why else did he need them back if he did not value them in the first place? How much would he pay for them? What would you trade for them? All they really wanted was their own ancestor's skeletons. Was it so hard to give them the right skeletons?

There was a lot of food for thought here. No wonder they were not able to get archaeologists to respect Native American ancestors, they did not respect their own ancestors.

How could the archaeologists not think of skeletons as

people or at least the representatives of souls? The question grieved him. Everyone he had ever met found the sight of a dead body disturbing. Some people found it terrifying, while others became distraught, but everyone reacted. It was a highly emotional experience. He could not fathom how this man could have no reaction or worse yet react with abject curiosity. Maybe he was figuratively blind and was unable to feel normal emotions..

Joe overheard Lilly say, "Go on in."

There was a polite rap at the door as a young man entered.

"Hi, I'm Eric Larson. I'm part of the tribe, and I need to talk to you."

"Come on in." Joe welcomed the interruption. "I'm always happy to help."

"I work at the museum," Eric said nervously. "You've requested that our ancestor's skeletons be returned."

"Yes, I sent a request." Joe felt like he was sinking. Not another person from the museum! He could not stand it. What was going on at this place?

"They can't return them," Eric stumbled. "They don't have them. I have them, sort of..."

Joe wondered if everyone involved there was crazy? "What exactly do you mean, you have them, sort of?"

"I didn't think they'd ever return them," Eric explained, "not ever, or I would have let them. I figured that if they didn't know the skeletons were gone, they'd never miss them. I'm the night watchman. Certainly the way I look, they'd never think I was half Wampanoag..."

Joe considered it and nodded. The point was well taken.

"So, I took them," Eric confessed. "I just walked out with them. They're safely and respectfully buried in Mother Earth. I'm not going to say where. So, you're not going to get them back, because they're already back."

It was beginning to make sense to Joe. He began to wonder if that meant he was crazy too.

"Won't you get into trouble?" Joe asked.

"Only if they find out..." Eric replied pointedly.

Joe almost laughed out loud. "Your intentions were good.

I'm not sure about your approach, but to say the least, it is unique and effective." He kept a professional image, but privately he loved the idea.

"I'll be leaving the area soon anyway..." Eric shrugged.

"So, what do you want me to do?" Joe was starting to feel like a broken record saying that.

" I don't really know," Eric said. He felt relieved just telling someone else. "Maybe drop the request. I just wanted you to know the truth for the people."

"This matter deserves some thought," Joe said solemnly. "I'm not going to make any snap decisions here."

"Here's my phone numbers," Eric said scribbling them down. "I gotta go pack." He waved as he left.

Joe tried to sort all of this out. What did he have here? A guy who secreted all of the Wampanoag bones away and buried them. An administrator frantically looking for them. An archaeologist whose bones are missing...

He surmised what was probably going on and laughed out loud. He found it truly humorous. No wonder everyone wanted him to drop the request. All of them deserved to sweat it out, at least for a little while. There was no way he was going to drop it, not yet.

One very important thing was missing in the picture. He had not received any official notification that these skeletons were being returned to him. That was interesting. There must be something else going on here. He was tempted to call up Dr. Moorland and find out what it was.

Then it hit him. He had a sudden strong urge to get out of the office. Not only that, he knew he needed to stay out of the office. It was an overwhelming feeling, and he decided to honor it. He had had a lot of them in his life, and they had never steered him wrong. Part of the feeling told him to leave no word about when he would be back. He packed up his more important business and left.

Chapter Nine

Ellen pouted, but it did not help. She stood aimlessly in front of Lilly's desk. "But I need to tell him in person," she whined. "Just this one time, it's terribly important. I worked so hard on the project."

"I really, truly don't know when he'll be back," Lilly explained calmly. She had been explaining or rather not explaining Joe's absence for days now. The whole matter was hardly her fault, but the explanation fell on her. She went into total automatic pilot when the question was asked.

"Can't you even tell him it's here?" Ellen persisted.

"No," Lilly said emphatically. "We've been over this. He isn't here, so I can't tell him anything."

"But this is **the** family!" Ellen objected. "I'm sure it's the one he's been looking for. I've got all of their phone numbers and addresses right here. I've been working on it so long, I'm sure he'll want it immediately."

"This is just like dialing the wrong number," Lilly said sternly. "No matter how many times you dial it, it is still the wrong number. Joe is not here, and he does not answer his phone. I don't know how to reach him or why he is gone."

"Can't you do anything?" Ellen pleaded.

"I can put it on his desk," Lilly enticed. In her head she planned where to prop it. "That's the fastest way to get it to him."

"Very well," Ellen sighed dejectedly. This was very disappointing. She was going to miss her chance to brag. This would be an exciting moment, but it would have to be exciting over the phone.

It was a gorgeous morning, and Joe took time to relax. Today he felt different. It was time to go back to work. He had gotten off to a late start, but it was for the best. Now he had his focus back.

It was strange that those museum people had such a disconcerting effect on him. Granted, he was not used to having people barge in and yell at him. It took him a couple of days off to recover, and that was weird.

He arrived at his office with his one allowed cup of Dunkin' Donuts coffee. He ignored Lilly's icy comments and started sorting through his desk. He opened Ellen's report and skimmed through it. He was so astonished by one of the names that he dumped the precious cup of coffee and did not even care.

What Soft Rain told Rad was astoundingly correct. When you pursue all avenues, things mysteriously start to work out. One of the heirs of one of the suspected thieves was Caleb Russell Emerson!

So he wanted to get his skeletons back? The Wampum belts were probably still in the Emerson Family's possession. There had to be a way to work out a trade.

Dr. Emerson seemed desperate. If Joe judged him properly, he would turn over the belts only if there were absolutely no other choice. Joe would need to take a hard line with him.

There was only one real difficulty. The eight Emerson skeletons were not actually in his possession yet. He had to think on that problem.

Susan simply did not understand. Initially, she presumed that finding these skeletons was a test. She thought that Moorland sincerely wanted her to find them. So, now that the skeletons were found and ready to go, why did he not acknowledge that? Did he want to fire her?

Monday had come and gone. There was not a word from him. What should she do? She certainly did not want to pester him. That would definitely put her on his bad side.

But, what was going on? Jeannie was noncommittal on the matter, but there was one other indirect way to find out. She called Joe Green.

"Hi, is Joe there? This is Susan Slater... yes, from the museum."

Joe was surprised to say the least. He did not want to get his hopes up, but this could be the opportunity he needed. "Nice to hear from you, Susan," he said affably. "How are you?"

"I'm fine thanks," she said brightly. "I'm so sorry I disturbed you the other day. I was just so tired that I was at the end of my rope."

"Oh, Susan, don't worry about it. It was nice to meet you, and I'm glad you're feeling better."

"I called to tell you," Susan said trying not to sound like she was fishing, "that I have all eight skeletons ready to be returned, paperwork and all."

"That's great!" Joe crossed his fingers. "You say you found eight Native American skeletons?"

"Yes, all eight," Susan replied proudly. "I searched and searched. Finally, I opened a box and there was a Native American skeleton. They were all right in a row. Once I found one, I had all of them."

"Good for you," Joe said happily.

"Has Dr. Moorland made arrangements with you to send the bones over to you yet?" Susan tried not to sound hesitant.

"No, not yet," Joe said with baited breath.

"Could you do me a favor?" Susan asked sweetly. "Could you call me when they arrive?"

"I suppose so, but why?"

"Dr. Moorland hired me." Susan had hoped to avoid this explanation. "Then he seemed to take a dislike to me. I can't imagine what I've done. He gave me this assignment and told me to hurry or else. Now, it's done, and he couldn't care less. I just don't understand."

"That is peculiar," Joe agreed. "I'll call you when I hear from him."

Susan thanked him and hung up. It was a disappointing conversation. What had she expected? She did not know, but it was more than what she got. There was nothing to do but sigh and go back to work.

After Joe hung up, he sat back to think the matter over. At

first he thought about Dr. Moorland and what his motives might be.

Was Dr. Moorland trying to fire Susan? Why would he do that? He had just hired her. She certainly seemed like a sincere person who was trying hard to do her job. Personally, Joe would work with an employee like that.

Was Dr. Moorland trying to be politically correct? Was he trying to avoid being politically correct? Was pressure being exerted on him from another party?

Then Joe realized this line of thinking was all wrong. It did not matter what anyone's intention was. These three people had opened the doors for him. That was what was important.

It was a glorious sunny afternoon. Because he worked at night, Eric was sleeping fitfully when he got the call.

"Hi, Eric, this is Joe Green."

"Ummm," Eric grunted.

Joe immediately realized he was interrupting a night's sleep. "I'm sorry to wake you."

"That's okay....," Eric muttered. "I guess."

"Maybe I should call back?"

"No," Eric said firmly. "I'm awake." Asking someone to call back only kept him awake wondering what they wanted. He might as well find out.

"You remember that matter you came to talk to me about?" Joe inquired slowly.

"About the ancestors?" Eric asked. He was still shaking off sleep.

"Exactly," Joe said bluntly. "I've found a way to straighten it all out."

"That's great!" Eric felt a sense of relief.

"But, I need your help," Joe told him. "You still work there don't you?"

"Yeah," Eric replied hesitantly. "For a few more days. Why do you ask?"

"Here's the plan," Joe said. "Could you tell Susan that Moorland asked you to take care of transferring the bones?

Would she release them to you?"

"Probably," Eric said. The idea worried him. "But, I'm not sure I should."

"She expects you to bring them to me," Joe explained. "Dr. Moorland told her that he was sending them to us. So that's what you'll do. You pick them up and bring them here. Trust me, it'll all work out."

"What about forms and stuff?" Eric asked anxiously.

"That's easy," Joe answered. "She has all of the paperwork. Just say that she's supposed to give the paperwork to you, and you'll give Moorland a copy."

Eric considered the matter uneasily. "Joe, I respect you and all," he said slowly. "But I don't know about doing this. I could get into a lot of trouble."

"This is cleaning up trouble," Joe assured, "not causing more. Besides, what do you care? You're leaving town anyway."

"That's true," Eric was almost convinced.

"The skeletons Susan has are not ours," Joe pointed out. "You know that better than anyone."

"What are you going to do with them?" Eric asked. This was a confusing matter, and he wished he was more awake to deal with it.

"Ultimately," Joe clarified easily. "I'm going to return them to their family. A member of the family contacted me, and he asked to make a trade."

Eric was starting to feel better about this. "Is he going to bury them?"

"Yes," Joe replied. "He said he's planning on it."

"I'm glad to hear that," Eric said quickly.

It was Joe's turn to be curious. "Why do you ask?"

"Because," Eric explained. "They might not officially be our ancestors, but one of them was very questionable. She's probably partly Native American. What happens to her has really been bothering me."

"That would explain some confusion," Joe replied thoughtfully. "Yes, they'll be properly buried. There's just one other thing."

"Can I go back to sleep after that?"

"Can you keep this whole matter absolutely confidential?" Joe requested.

"I will if you will," Eric yawned.

After they hung up, Joe pondered on the partly Native American skeleton. It was entirely possible that despite his blue blood, Dr. Emerson had some Native American heritage. Virtually every old New England family did whether they admitted it or not.

It very well could explain Susan's mistake. One of the skeletons looked Native American. Maybe that was the only one she checked closely. It was exactly the kind of mistake that someone would make if they were tired and distraught.

It was funny. Suddenly, so many little things were working in his favor. Would they work out? He felt like holding his breath.

Susan felt dejected and insecure. There were still eight boxes cluttering up her office. So far, she had not heard anything from Dr. Moorland. She was not sure if that was good or bad. Maybe she should just be happy that he had not fired her yet.

The telephone rang.

"Hi, Susan, this is Joe Green. How are you?"

"I'm okay," Susan said happily. "How are you?"

"Just fine," Joe replied politely. "You said to call you when I heard something."

"What's going on?" Susan asked eagerly.

"We're getting our ancestors' skeletons back today," Joe told her pleasantly. "I called to thank you for all of your help and hard work."

"You're welcome," Susan replied cordially. "I'm pleased to hear it's all working out."

As they hung up, Susan was beginning to feel quite pleased with herself. Maybe all of her worry was for nothing. The problem with Dr. Moorland might be communication. Perhaps she ought to presume she had passed his little test.

Eric appeared in her door. "Susan, I'm here to pick up those boxes of bones." He tried to act casual.

"You are?" Susan said with surprise. "These aren't your usual hours. Why are you awake?"

Eric shrugged to cover the lie. "Dr. Moorland told me if I felt like putting in a couple of extra hours to come and pick them up."

"Okay," Susan said agreeably. "I'll remember to approve it on your time sheet." She decided to fish for more information. "How come no one said anything to me about you coming to pick them up?"

"I don't know," Eric shrugged again nervously. "It's like that around here sometimes."

"Did Dr. Moorland say anything to you about paperwork?" Susan asked. She wanted to show off her new forms.

"Oh, yeah, he said you'd have it," Eric stumbled. He hated lying, even for a good cause. "And he said to bring him a copy after I dropped the load off."

"That's good," Susan said riffling through her desk. "Here it is." She handed him her new transfer forms. "Help yourself to the boxes."

Eric silently breathed a sigh of relief. Quickly, he picked up a box and headed for the door.

As Eric drove away with the skeletons, he wondered about what he was doing. It seemed to him that taking away more skeletons would made the situation even more confusing.

On the other hand, Joe was keeping his secret. Eric felt he could trust Joe to act in the best interest of the tribe. Eric couldn't see how this would all balance out. But he decided to have faith and keep Joe's confidence as he wanted Joe to keep his.

Joe had a plan, and he had a meeting. He had spent hours trying to prepare for it. After careful thought, he positioned the eight museum boxes of skeletons somewhat conspicuously in the corner. It was a little grotesque but necessary.

This was going to be a tough meeting. It was his nature to negotiate, and today it was very important that he refuse to compromise at all.

Dr. Emerson came in and noted the eight familiar museum boxes in the corner before he sat down. He was a little anxious, because he was not sure what to expect. The voice mail message had been cryptic to say the least.

"You talked about a trade," Joe said directly. "I have one for you."

"What's that?" Caleb asked curiously.

"You have the Wampum Belts," Joe spoke firmly. "We want them back."

"Wampum Belts?" Caleb asked absently. How could Joe know about that? In the attic there were a pile of Indian relics. There had always been a rumor in the family that some of them were extremely valuable. He had never believed in it enough to investigate.

"The Wampum Belts," Joe said sternly. "The ones stolen from us during King Philip's war."

"We have some Indian artifacts," Caleb admitted. Inside he was aghast. How could this Indian possibly know about that? "But, I seriously doubt..."

"Don't deny it," Joe snapped harshly. "I know how your family came by them, and I don't want to address that. The deal is this, after you return all of the Native American relics you inherited, I'll see that you get your bones back."

"Wouldn't you prefer money?" Caleb offered lamely.

"No," Joe replied flatly. "We want our relics back."

"But," Caleb objected. "There'll be questions..."

"An anonymous donation, naturally."

"Just exactly which artifacts do you want?" Caleb requested dubiously. There might just be a way to get around the worst of this.

"All of them," Joe said hotly. He looked Caleb right in the eye angrily. "If I find you've held out as much as a broken arrowhead from a souvenir shop, I'll let my account of this whole matter drop into a reporter's hands."

"That's the deal?" Caleb winced, wondering just how much Joe knew. Maybe he could get eight skeletons elsewhere.

"There's one other little matter," Joe added. He might as well go for everything. "That new woman, Susan,"

"What about her?" Caleb asked.

"I might be dropping a hint to her about this," Joe said pointedly. "It would be a good idea to help her out, so that she gets and stays on Moorland's good side."

"That's easy enough," Dr. Emerson replied. He was beginning to deeply resent this whole situation. "It's the relics that are the problem, you see, they aren't actually mine."

"Work it out," Joe ordered harshly. Then he changed his tone to nonchalant. "You came to me and asked for a deal. This is the only deal you're going to get. If you'd prefer, I'll keep these skeletons and forgot the whole matter."

"No," Caleb replied bitterly. Giving away anything, especially something valuable, rubbed him the wrong way, but he was up against the wall. "I'll figure it out."

When the premonition hit, Melissa dropped the payroll problem she was working on. Steve was coming home tonight! She absolutely knew it!

Immediately, she called Eric, and then she called their parents. Neither one was home, so she left them the same message. "Rad is returning tonight. You have to come over and help me put the plan into action. Be at my house by six. Dinner's on me!"

Caleb went through the chest in the attic. All of the Indian relics were in here. Of course, so was a lot of other junk. There were a lot of Wampum belts here. He toyed with the idea of holding out King Philip's Wampum Belts. They had not been seen for three hundred years. Would anyone know the real ones from substitutes?

Well, that was the other problem. He would eventually have to come up with something to say to his family. They all knew that some of the relics in the attic were rumored to be King Philip's Wampum Belts.

The rumor was the sort of thing you passed through the family but never took seriously or publicized. The relics were still kicking around, because if they were fake no one wanted to know.

Also there was the question of who actually owned them. Possession was nine tenths of the law, but legally, the British Crown owned them. The Belts should have been turned over to King Charles II immediately as spoils of war. Naturally, the Wampanoags would put in a claim, but he had never taken that seriously. They did not have much clout. Worse yet, they might forbid study and treat them as holy. He had never realized they were so emotional about it. Could one set of relics mean that much to them?

To him, they were just another artifact. Today was Friday, and insuring his inheritance was much more important than preserving rumors. If it ever came up, he could say the relics were valueless, so he donated them to the museum for a tax deduction. No one would question that in the family. Tax deductions were always smiled upon.

Caleb packed up the relics including King Philip's Wampum Belts and drove directly to Joe's office with them. He ignored the annoyed secretary and gave the belts directly to Joe.

While Caleb waited impatiently, Joe inspected the Belts with reverence. They were dazzling! The colors of the shells were brilliant. Each design was part of a story. He repeated the stories aloud, laying them out in order. They were correct and complete.

"I believe," Joe pronounced solemnly. "They are possibly authentic, but I will have to present them to the Elders."

Caleb thought he was going to blow a fuse. This was ridiculous. He was out of time! "Authentication might never be settled," he protested.

"I'll see to that matter," Joe said still entranced with the belts. "Consider it settled."

Caleb was not used to being dismissed this way. "Well," he demanded impatiently. "May I have my skeletons now?"

"Absolutely," Joe said looking up. He motioned at the corner with his head. "They're all yours."

Caleb picked up the first box grumbling slightly to himself. He had expected at least to be offered help carrying them out.

"Oh, don't forget about Susan," Joe reminded amiably.

Rad arrived home anticipating a big welcome. He had been gone a long time. Probably, there had been a lot of publicity and worry. Certainly, his return would be a big surprise.

He did not quite know what he expected from Melissa. Maybe he wanted her to be mad at him. Maybe he wanted her to be happy to see him. Naturally, he wanted her to be impressed with his daring accomplishment. But he definitely did not expect to be totally ignored.

"Melissa," Rad called from the kitchen doorway. "Sweetheart, I'm home!"

"Hi, Steve," Melissa called back from the other room. "There's leftovers in the fridge."

Rad waited, feeling a little miffed, but she did not come into the kitchen to see him. After a minute, he ventured into the living room to find Melissa, Eric, and their parents playing cards.

"Hey, Rad," Eric greeted him. His in-laws waved briefly, and then they went back to concentrating on their game.

"I did it," Rad announced proudly. "The Hillman Plan, did you hear?"

"I have to trump that," Melissa announced, sweeping in a pile of cards.

"So, that's where that ace was," Eric said knowingly.

"Was it in the newspaper?" Rad interjected hopefully.

"So you had all the trump," Melissa said to her dad.

"Don't you want to hear what I did?" Rad asked wonderingly. He was starting to feel a little dejected. "I've been away all this time..."

"I miscounted," Eric said to his dad. "You had that last one."

"Better luck next hand," his dad said shuffling the cards.

Steve waited expectantly for a minute. Then he trudged into the kitchen to heat up dinner.

After Steve left the room, Eric started to smile. Melissa looked away to keep from laughing. Both parents kept straight faces, but their eyes twinkled. By the time they finished the hand, they were all giggling.

Joe sprawled in his easy chair. It had been a long full day. He was ready to pat himself on the back. It seemed unreal to him. He had the Wampum Belts! After all this time and effort, they were finally back with the people.

There was a fire burning, and he was tired. Despite the time of year, it was chilly tonight. The flickering light made him doze off. He awakened with a start. What was he thinking about? He had not called Ellen. She was largely responsible for finding them. Of all people, she ought to know, but what should he tell her?

Would she keep the identity of the contributor confidential? It was the nature of the work, but this was a very big issue. Could he trust her? He did not know.

Grudgingly, he admitted to himself that he had less faith in her, because she was White. He presumed her first loyalty would probably be with herself, not the Wampanoags. If she could get publicity for her discovery, she would, and for that, the more details, the better.

He knew being White did not necessarily mean a person was untrustworthy. There were a few members of his own tribe he would not trust as far as he could throw them. Just the same, past experience biased him.

He decided to play it safe. If you don't want it told, then don't tell it, his grandmother used to say.

He had not promised complete confidence to Caleb Emerson, but certainly, he had implied it since exposure had worked as a threat. Yes, he was obliged to keep the secret.

So, what to tell Ellen? An anonymous donation would solve the whole problem. Maybe it was a coincidence, and maybe they had struck a chord. They would never know for certain.

Ellen reclined on the couch swirling a glass of wine. What to do next? She wondered if she was done with the Wampanoag cases. It would be nice to hear from Joe. If the case was finished, she should start advertising to scare up more business. Advertising was expensive, so she did not want to run ads unless it was necessary.

"Hi, Ellen, I hope it's not too late to call," Joe said.

"Not at all," Ellen replied. "I was just thinking about you. What's going on?"

"Well, I have very big news," Joe announced. "The Wampum Belts have been anonymously returned!"

"By the Emerson-Loring Family?" Ellen asked eagerly.

"Hard to say," Joe said carefully. He disliked lying. "It was anonymous."

"It has to be them." Ellen said jubilantly. "Otherwise, it's too big a coincidence to be believed."

"Officially, you understand, I can't presume anything," Joe explained. "It would be a bizarre coincidence, but it could happen."

"But, we know it must have been the Emersons!" Ellen exclaimed happily.

"It probably was," Joe conceded. "Probably, they got my message and decided to turn them over before their family name was involved. But, it's possible there was a distant relation or a friend or even an acquaintance they happened to mention it to and..."

"I never thought of that!" Ellen interjected. "Politics have changed with the times. Maybe they wanted to avoid a scandal."

"A good assumption," Joe said. It was true, and he felt comfortable with that. "I wish we could attribute it to someone specific. It would be better for both of us."

"We've got what we wanted," Ellen pointed out. "I'm elated about it!"

"So am I," Joe agreed. "This will mean more to the People than you can ever know."

"The project is a success!"

"You did a fine job, Ellen," Joe said heartily. "I'll expect your final bill next week."

"I'm sorry it's over," Ellen said sincerely. "This has been a fascinating project."

"You'll get a great reference from us," Joe assured her. "Besides, if there's ever a Wampanoag in the family tree, maybe our tribal roles will helpful to you."

"Thank you," Ellen said. "If and when I get another case, I'll take you up on that offer."

"Then I'll be seeing you, thanks again." Joe hung up, feeling that conversation had not been too painful.

Ellen gathered up the Wampanoag files and dropped them on her desk with a loud thunk. What a huge amount of extraneous work she had done. What a shame it was going to go to waste. Then she thought of a way to use it. All she had to do was find the descendants and sell them the family trees she had already traced.

"I really should go out and talk to him," Melissa giggled. "Should we all go?"

"No, dear," their mother said. "We're going home. We've had about enough for tonight."

"You can fill us in tomorrow," their father added. They got up and headed to the door.

"What about you, Eric?" Melissa asked. "You should stay."

"Ummm," Eric replied thoughtfully. "I'll stay out here and put the cards away for now. Call when you want me."

Melissa walked her parents to the door. Then she went to the kitchen to see her husband.

Steve was sulking at the kitchen table eating leftover chicken and rice. He was very disappointed in his homecoming. Getting home from work got him more attention than this.

"Hi, Honey," Melissa called softly. She walked up behind him and kissed his cheek. "Where you been all this time?"

"I was wondering if you noticed." He kept on eating and sulking.

"You worried me sick," Melissa told him sharply. "If it hadn't been for Eric distracting me, I would have had a complete meltdown."

Rad looked up hopefully. "Really?"

"Yes, really!" She faked a punch to his ear and pretended to strangle him. "How could you do that to me? I almost had a nervous break down! What did you do?"

He laughed and gave her a kiss. "Wait till you hear about

this! I made a great political statement."

Melissa sat down next to him and waited expectantly.

"I had to protest the museum holding our ancestors' skeletons," Rad explained proudly, "so I dug up one of their ancestor's skeletons. It was great! I went practically into the guy's backyard and dug up a grave. Then I mailed him the bones, so he could see how we feel about it."

Melissa gasped. "You really were waiting for the FBI to show up at the door!"

"Yeah, was it in the paper?"

"Not that I read about," Melissa said. Her feelings had been right. He could be in a lot of trouble. "We've got to tell Eric about this."

She got up and went around the corner and motioned to him.

Eric came in the kitchen. "So, what's up?"

"Wait until you hear this!" Melissa exclaimed. "Of all the things he's ever done, this is the most radical."

"That's why they call me Rad!" Steve bragged.

"So, let's hear," Eric said.

"I decided to give those museum bigwigs a taste of their own medicine. I went to one of their grand estates and dug up a body from their own backyard. Then I mailed it to them at the museum!"

"Wow!" was all Eric could say. He was impressed. Rad had really done something after all. "What made you think to do that?"

"Well, it's not very original." Steve made a face. "Some guy did it in the book, 'Talking God'. That's why I called it the 'Hillman Plan'."

"Who was the target?" Eric asked. "Remember, I might know them."

"That should've made the papers!" Melissa exclaimed. "Eric, you must've heard about it."

"No," Eric said. "I can't believe it!"

"I sent it to Dr. Caleb Russell Emerson," Rad said proudly.

"I know him," Eric said.

"Was he shocked?" Rad asked eagerly.

"Not that I could tell," Eric replied. "He's pretty

closemouthed about his personal life though."

"Has he at least been acting strangely?" Rad asked anxiously. "As though he was upset?"

"No," Eric replied thoughtfully. He wanted to tell Rad about the other skeletons, but he had to keep his promise to Joe. "He hasn't been any stranger than he usually is. He's been working a lot, and if anything, he's more cheerful."

"Maybe he didn't get it," Melissa suggested.

"I can't believe it," Rad said dismally. "I damn near broke my back for nothing."

"Not quite," Melissa said. "We haven't told you what we've been up to."

"You inspired it," Eric added.

"What'd you do?" Steve asked. He could not imagine them doing anything related to his usual endeavors at all. Generally, Eric came along for laughs, and Melissa stressed out.

"You know those eight Wampanoag skeletons the museum was holding?" Melissa baited to build suspense.

"The focus of my protest!" Rad said impatiently. "Yeah, what about them?"

"Their new resting place," Melissa announced slowly, "is our back field."

"What!" Rad was dumbfounded. "How?"

"I walked off with them from work," Eric explained, grinning ear to ear. "It was cool."

"He brought them back here," Melissa continued. "And, we gave them a traditional funeral."

Rad looked from one to the other. How could this be? All of the times and all of the causes he had protested, demonstrated, and crusaded for had come to little or nothing. These two quietly, almost inadvertently, succeeded where he had, well, failed.

Chapter Ten

Dr. Emerson knocked on Susan's office door and entered. He looked around at her set up with the lamps and screens. Now that she had her own decor inside, it was rather tasteful.

Susan was certainly surprised. In the time she had worked there, Dr. Emerson still had not said more than a dozen words to her. Something must be wrong.

"Susan," Dr. Emerson said briskly. "Are you going to be reporting to Joshua soon?"

"Yes," Susan replied. "I expect so. Why?"

"Hummh," Dr. Emerson groused. "Well, what are you going to say to him?"

"Usually," Susan explained frankly. "I give him a rundown on what's been going on."

"Do you give him the specifics?" Dr. Emerson asked testily.

"Yes, of course," Susan said immediately. What was his interest in it?

"That's all wrong," Dr. Emerson snapped. "He doesn't want to hear that." Her problem was that she was oblivious. No wonder Joshua was not happy with her. "If you do that, he'll get annoyed with you."

"Thanks for the advice," Susan said tentatively. Was that what she was doing wrong?

"On Monday, stop by my office," Dr. Emerson ordered. From the look on her face, she needed guidance. "We should go over a few things about the position and how to handle Joshua."

"Thank you," Susan said sincerely. If there was anything she needed it was advice on handling Joshua. "I appreciate it." This was too good to be true. Things were shaping up.

"Hurng," Dr. Emerson grumbled. He left abruptly leaving Susan to puzzle over why he had stopped in the first place.

Ellen was settled in her favorite carrel at the local historical society. Carefully, she rolled through the microfilm. The census index named a member of the family she was after. It was just a matter of perseverance to find them.

She might as well relax. None of her cases were active. The family she was tracing was one of the Wampanoag File families. She was no longer on Joe's payroll, but the families she had traced might be interested in what she had found. There could be a buck in it, and there was no sense in wasting good research.

"Pssst," she heard a voice over the wall of the carrel. "Can you give me a hand?"

Ellen looked over the wall and saw a very handsome man fumbling with film.

"I'd be happy to," she said quickly clicking the reel into place. "My name is Ellen."

"I'm Dave," he said, smiling flirtatiously. "I'm just muddling around here."

"Are you just starting to research your family?" Ellen asked. He had a charming smile.

"Sort of..." Dave answered. He decided to explain in order to make conversation. "My sister started the project. Then she had another baby and got too busy. There was one branch she lost, so I'm taking a stab at looking for them."

"I do genealogy professionally," Ellen said thoughtfully. "Why did she lose them?"

"I'm not sure," Dave said hesitantly. He decided he might as well tell her. She seemed nice. "There's a glitch way back in the family tree. My sister thinks it's because they were Wampanoag Indians."

"Would you consider hiring someone?" Ellen asked. This would be a great way to get to know him. "I have some very good connections with the Wampanoags. In fact, I just finished a project with them."

"I'd consider hiring you," Dave said warmly. "I had no idea how time consuming this is. How about if I take you out for dinner tonight, so we can talk about it?"

"I'd love to," Ellen agreed happily.

The Elders looked on with awe at the display of King Philip's Wampum Belts. Joe beamed proudly at the outcome of his project. He listened to the stream of comments.

"The pictures follow the stories exactly."

"Not quite like my grandfather told it, but very close."

"That's the way my grandfather told it. They always did disagree."

"An anonymous donation - after all this time. Can they be real?"

"Should we consider dating them?"

"Can dating be done without damaging them?"

"What date do we accept? They may be three hundred years old, and they may be a thousand years old. We should be going by content."

Joe stood by waiting for some consensus. So many things had come into play here. First there was Rad's crazy stunt, digging up a grave. Then there was Eric quietly reclaiming his ancestors. The whole genealogical coincidence itself was amazing. Even more amazing was that all this had converged upon him at exactly the right time.

As though she could hear his thoughts, Soft Rain looked over at him and nodded. Her inspection had consisted of running her hands over the belts and proclaiming them authentic. She stood aside, quietly waiting for the others to finish.

The debating continued. What had he expected? At an emotional level, he had already accepted them on a leap of faith. But that was easy, because he knew the origins of the belts. The Elders did not know the background, and he did not feel he could tell them the whole story.

Just having possible Wampum Belts was a huge boost in morale for the whole tribe. The origin of the Belts made Joe believe they were authentic. Still, for some people even that would not be enough. It was better to let them come to acceptance on their own terms. Knowing that they were authentic made him have faith, and after all, that had worked so far.

Joshua Moorland overlooked Susan's report with

satisfaction. There were no problems whatsoever. Everything was neat and concise. Obviously she was getting along well with Caleb. She scrawled, "See you at the clambake," at the bottom of the report.

This was excellent. There was no mention of system problems or moving relics or relics being given away. She did mention a routine upcoming personnel replacement. Ah, good, she had caught on. This saved him a personnel replacement.

Melissa and Steve stood by while Eric checked his luggage. Holding his plane ticket nervously, he walked back over to them.

"I guess this is it..." Eric mumbled. Good-byes were always difficult. He wished he felt more confident about the move and Astrid and fatherhood.

Melissa hugged him. "Eric, I'm going to miss you. I just hope it all works out for you."

"I hope Astrid accepts this diamond," Eric said worriedly. "If she doesn't, Sis, maybe I'll see you sooner, right?"

"Don't say that," Melissa consoled. "She'll love it. I'm not used to thinking of you as a family man, but I'm sure you'll be really happy together."

"Hey, man," Rad said, slapping him on the shoulder. "I'm proud of you. When you saw the chance, you moved right in and made things right. You're doing the right thing here, too."

"Thanks Rad," Eric said seriously. "You inspired me. Y'know, I look up to you."

"Hey, I gotta live up to that now," Rad protested.

Both the guys hit each other again. Melissa gave Eric one last kiss.

"Bye, Rad. Bye, Sis! I'll miss you!" Eric called as he walked up the ramp.

Caleb was busy filling in graves. Fortunately, he was in good condition, because Mother insisted they all be done today.

Meg sat overlooking the project in a lawn chair. She was attired symbolically in black. A tumbler of Scotch and water sat beside her as she examined the newspaper.

"I see here," she sniffed, "there's been a local relic returned anonymously to these native people."

Caleb kept digging. His face burned. She just had to see that article, didn't she?

"What kind of an idiot," Meg asked snidely, "knowing the value of such a thing, would donate it anonymously?"

Caleb resisted the urge to throw dirt on her. "Maybe there's more to it than meets the eye."

"What does that mean?" Meg snapped. She added more Scotch to her drink. Her drinks always got darker as the day progressed.

"Mother," he said testily. "That means that sometimes the papers don't get the entire story. Sometimes they even get it totally wrong."

"That's true," she conceded. "Still, they should have held out for something in return. You should always get at least recognition for a substantial donation."

Caleb continued digging and filling. He desperately hoped she would drop the subject.

"Personally," Meg continued in her high handed tone. "I would have donated them to a museum, if I were to donate them, which is unlikely. They should have been assessed, certainly. At least, a tax break could have been negotiated. Do you know about dating such things?"

"Naturally," Caleb replied, desperately trying to change the subject. "But you know I don't specialize in local archaeology. My preferred fields..."

"Apparently," Meg interrupted bluntly. "This was that beaded stuff the Indians around here made before discovery. I can't see it having any other value. I believe there was some of that floating around the attic at one time."

Caleb continued shoveling diligently. This was a good chance to explain the relics' absence, so he jumped at it. "I donated all that to the museum some years ago. It was excellent for a tax deduction, because there was absolutely no market value for it."

"Of course, you did well," Meg said proudly. "You know

how to capitalize on such things. I pride myself on having taught all of you children financial savvy. None of you would miss an opportunity like that."

"Of course not, Mother," Caleb chimed as he shoveled. He could not stand it. This time he did throw dirt on her.

Author's Note

As of this writing, the Wampanoags have not received national recognition, and the whereabouts of the Wampum Belts remain a mystery. Hopefully, those situations will eventually improve.

Thanks to authors Tony Hillerman and Charles Turek Robinson whose works inspired my imagination.

About the Author

Katherine Traphagen has written two novels, "Anomaly Adventures" and "Skeletal Scramble," as well as a screenplay, "Nice To Meet You."

Originally from Erie, Pennsylvania, she lived in Boston, Massachusetts for fifteen years. She graduated from Michigan State University in 1982.

Ms. Traphagen's main career has been Blood Banking. She has also forayed into genealogy, real estate, and tarot card reading.